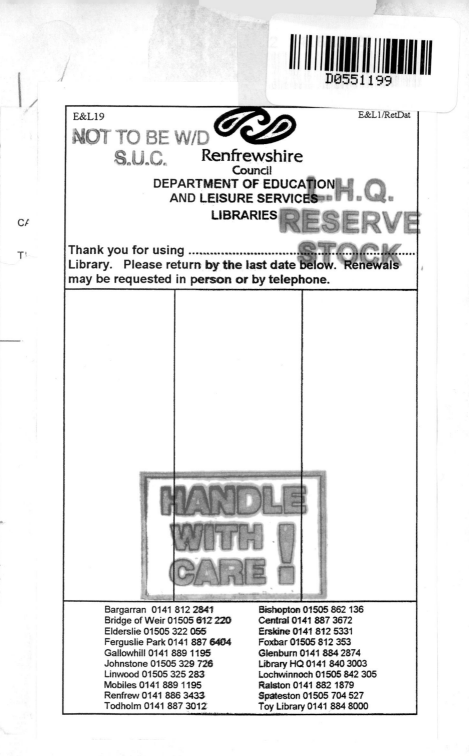

FAMOUS REGIMENTS

The King's Royal Rifle Corps

FAMOUS REGIMENTS

EDITED BY

LT.-GENERAL SIR BRIAN HORROCKS

The King's Royal Rifle Corps

(The 60th Regiment of Foot)

BY

HERBERT FAIRLIE WOOD

HAMISH HAMILTON
LONDON

First published in Great Britain 1967
by Hamish Hamilton Ltd
90 Great Russell Street London W.C.1
Copyright © 1967 by Herbert Wood
Introduction Copyright © 1967 by Lt.-General Sir Brian Horrocks

Printed in Great Britain
by Ebenezer Baylis and Son, Limited
The Trinity Press, Worcester, and London

FOREWORD

TIME WAS NOT given to my husband to write of his
thanks to those who helped and advised him in his research: he died within a few days of finishing the manu-
script. I know he thanked them personally. He gave of his
best to do justice to the subject and to do it within the
period specified in his contract, and he was glad that that
which he set out to do was found to be acceptable. This
reaction is that of a professional soldier and a professional
writer: he was rare in that he was both.

All his non-fiction recorded the deeds of others and
added to the knowledge of Canadian history specifically
and British history generally. As a brother officer of his
wrote me, in doing this he left his own memorial. Thus it
was typical and fitting that his last work should record the
history of a regiment raised in the continent where he was
born and brought up and belonging to the country from
which his forebears came and gave their loyalty, and where
he finally chose to rest.

His editor, Leo Cooper, became his friend on first
acquaintance. As a publisher he did rather more than either
of us had the right to expect—in getting the work out on
schedule, and much more beside.

Brigadier Peter Curtis helped with introductions and
background material and was well aware, through military
and family relationship, of my husband's eagerness to
catch and put on paper the spirit of the Regiment.

The Depot in Winchester were kind—and that is an
understatement. Colonel Roger Nixon gave enthusiastic
encouragement and knowledge to forward the research,
and visited us at some geographical inconvenience when
illness prevented us from going to Winchester again.

Major Cyril Wilson also gave research help and, again, time. They gave these things after as well as before Herbert's death: for this I record my own thanks, and it extends to all those who helped to see the deadline was met, and properly. Major Christopher Hinton and Brigadier T. I. Dun did rather more than perhaps either of them ever knew on a visit we paid to Winchester in February of this year.

The Imperial War Museum, in whose Library Herbert had long felt at home, were most helpful not only with advice but with the loan of illustrations.

And finally, thanks go to Graham Watson of Curtis Brown. After I left the employ of that firm to marry one of 'my authors' (literary agents, as well as publishers, speak possessively in the book trade) he looked after Herbert's literary work. Herbert respected him and his skill and he was duly grateful, not for the first time, when the invitation to write this book arrived.

I asked Herbert to whom he would dedicate it. He felt the dedication should not be to an individual: that would have been invidious and regiments are corporate things, belonging to the past and to the future. He wondered about the Regiment as it was and as it is—and the service which lies ahead. 'Perhaps', he said, 'just The Regiment.'

The book itself is its own dedication, but

To The Regiment

it shall be.

JULIET WOOD
Cranleigh, July, 1967.

INTRODUCTION TO THE SERIES

by

LT.-GENERAL SIR BRIAN HORROCKS

IT IS ALWAYS sad when old friends depart. In the last few years many famous old regiments have disappeared, merged into larger formations.

I suppose this is inevitable; strategy and tactics are always changing, forcing the structure of the Army to change too. But the memories of the past still linger in minds now trained to great technical proficiency and surrounded by sophisticated equipment. Nevertheless the disappearance of these well-known names as separate units marks the end of a military epoch; but we must never forget that, throughout the years, each of these regiments has carved for itself a special niche in British History. The qualities of the British character, both good and bad, which helped England to her important position in the world can be seen at work in the regiments of the old Army. To see why these regiments succeeded under Marlborough and Wellington yet failed in the American War of Independence should help us in assessing the past.

Though many Battle Honours were won during historic campaigns, the greatest contribution which our Regiments have made to the British Empire is rarely mentioned: this has surely been the protection they have afforded to those indomitable British merchants, who in search of fresh markets spread our influence all over the world. For some of these this involved spending many years in stinking garrisons overseas where their casualties from disease were often far greater than those suffered on active service.

7

The main strength of our military system has always lain in the fact that regimental roots were planted deep into the British countryside in the shape of the Territorial Army, whose battalions are also subject to the cold winds of change. This ensured the closest possible link between civilian and military worlds, and built up a unique County and family *esprit de corps* which exists in no other Army in the world. A Cockney regiment, a West Country regiment and a Highland regiment differed from each other greatly, though they fought side by side in scores of battles. In spite of miserable conditions and savage discipline, a man often felt he belonged within the regiment—he shared the background and the hopes of his fellows. That was a great comfort for a soldier. Many times, at Old Comrades' gatherings, some old soldier has come up to me and said, referring to one of the World Wars, 'They were good times, sir, weren't they?'

They were not good times at all. They were horrible times; but what these men remember and now miss was the comradeship and *esprit de corps* of the old regular regiments. These regiments, which bound men together and helped them through the pain and fear of war, deserve to be recalled.

Regimental histories are usually terribly dull, as the authors are forced to record the smallest operation and include as many names as possible. In this series we have something new. Freed from the tyranny of minute detail, the authors have sought to capture that subtle quarry, the regimental spirit. The history of each regiment is a story of a type of British life now fading away. These stories illuminate the past, and should help us to think more clearly about the military future.

THE KING'S ROYAL RIFLE CORPS

A Special Introduction

by

LT.-GENERAL SIR BRIAN HORROCKS

ALMOST ALL BRITISH Infantry Regiments develop
their own family *esprit de corps* but over the years
the 60th and their fellow 'Black Buttons', The Rifle
Brigade, have become one of the most exclusive family
regiments in the military world. No one could hope to
become an officer in the 60th without close family con-
nections, and even then only after most searching inquiries
had been made by the Colonel Commandant of the Regiment. It is more difficult to obtain a commission in this
Regiment than in any other corps in the army including
the Household Cavalry, Cavalry, or Guards.

As a young officer I can remember well how infuriating
it was to have a 'Black Button' Battalion anywhere near
one on a ceremonial parade because without any warning
the band would suddenly accelerate to almost double time,
thus causing chaos in our well-ordered ranks, with everyone suddenly out of step.

For this reason and because of their extreme clannish-
ness (I prefer this word to snobbishness) in those days I
did not care for the Green Jackets very much. Later on, as
I grew older and I hope wiser, I came to realize that it was
precisely because of these qualities that they were such a
highly efficient regiment. The quick-step influenced their
whole way of thinking—the tempo of their lives was faster
than in the ordinary battalion and the tight family circle

9

embraced the youngest recruit from the moment he arrived at the Regimental Depot in Winchester. This had to be because throughout history they have always been given the most difficult and dangerous job in war, armed reconnaissance in front of the main line of battle which requires quick thinking, mobility, and mutual confidence.

Between the wars their mobile role after the static fighting of 1914–18 was restored by close co-operation with Armoured Formations in Support Groups, motor battalions, and so on, with the result that in the last war they really came into their own, particularly in the wide open desert. They were the backbone of those famous 'Jock Columns' which usually consisted of a motor company of Black Buttons plus some guns manned by The R.H.A. and a varying number of armoured cars. These were used for wide envelopments round the enemy's flank involving deep reconnaissance and raids on their communications, operations which involved long periods of hard living meticulous navigation and the capacity to act quickly. It was no job for amateurs, but the 60th have always been highly professional in this type of warfare.

When I arrived in the VIII Army during the third week of August 1942 to take command of the XIII Corps, I found that almost the whole of my southern flank was defended by Green Jackets including the 1st and 2nd K.R.R.C. widely dispersed in platoon positions along the minefields, and it was against this part of my front that Rommel's final onslaught to capture Egypt was likely to be launched.

It was a difficult time for me because the previous commander of XIII Corps had been 'Straffer' Gott, a 60th officer himself and one of the most popular and famous commanders in the desert. I doubt whether the bronzed lean, experienced desert veterans viewed the arrival of the new boy with painfully white knees from the U.K. with much enthusiasm, but they gave me a feeling of great confidence which was subsequently justified. It was largely due to the skill and tenacity with which they carried out a phased withdrawal in face of the German and Italian Armoured Division which upset Rommel's timings and caused him to lose the Battle of Alam Halfa.

From then on until the end of the war there were always some Green Jackets present in every action with which I was concerned. When I returned to the war in Europe after a period in hospital to command XXX Corps in the B.L.A. the 12th Battalion K.R.R.C. (2nd Battalion The Queen's Westminsters) working with the independent 8th Armoured Brigade took part in that rapid advance from the Seine when we covered 250 miles in six days. This was real motor battalion stuff which I am glad to say culminated, in the liberation of Brussels when we received a fantastic welcome the memory of which still brings a blush to the cheeks of the most hardened warrior even today.

At one time there were six battalions of the Regiment. Now there is only one, the 2nd Battalion of the Royal Green Jackets, but when announcing the amalgamation, their Commanding Officer said 'In this life if you are sensible and particularly if you are young, you look forward and not back'. This is typical of the attitude of the Green Jackets throughout their long history.

They have always looked forward.

Chapter One

We shall learn better how to do it the next time.

MAJ.-GEN. EDWARD BRADDOCK

THE 60TH OF FOOT, The King's Royal Rifle Corps, traces its origins back to the early adventures of European Powers in North America. That vast and empty continent had, from the time of the first discoveries, attracted the attention of every Maritime nation in Europe, and their settlements, dedicated to perpetuating, in the New World, the cherished values of the Old, had sprung up all along the coastlines.

The outbreak of the Seven Years War, in 1756, had repercussions across the Atlantic, for the European struggle could be influenced by the capture of bits of forest land 3,000 miles away. Spain and Portugal, predominant in the southern hemisphere, owned Caribbean islands too, while France, Holland and Great Britain had carved out colonies from Newfoundland to Louisiana.

Holland succumbed early in the competition, and when New Amsterdam became New York, the struggle for hegemony over the mainland became the preoccupation of France and Britain. Both sides sought the aid of the savage tribes which had been found in possession when the first discoveries were made. Called 'Indians' by early explorers who thought they had arrived in the land of the Moguls, their familiarity with the trackless forests beyond the coasts made them invaluable, if unpredictable, allies. The frontier bickering that characterized the Seven Years War in North America was always complicated by the Indians. Whatever notion of fair play they entertained did not include civilized

13

behaviour on the battlefield; Indian participation in the border wars usually resulted in burned farms, raped and tortured women, mutilated and murdered men. Inevitably, some of the savagery rubbed off on the white adversaries; the annals of the period are redolent with violence.

Many attempts were made to impose European ways of war; each attempt was frustrated by the wilderness. The stately minuets of disciplined armies, taught to manœuvre in a familiar environment, were not possible in a country where the field of fire was the length of one's musket and an army could be concealed in a forested area the size of a football field. In America, attempts to follow regulations written in Whitehall or Versailles brought swift catastrophe.

The French learned this lesson first. They were, for the most part, fur traders, their settlements merely bases secured against attack. The English, on the other hand, had come to stay. Long before the outbreak of the Seven Years War, the English hold on the Atlantic coast was agrarian and expansive. The colonists looked beyond the next range of hills for land to be tilled by their young. The French, by contrast, looked for wealth to take back home. This is an over-simplification, of course; there were many English fur-traders, and many French farmers. But, in general, the French explored for wealth while the English found it in their fields, livestock, and primitive industries.

Each side eyed the unknown interior acquisitively, determined that the other should not gain control of it, and as opportunity offered, both sides built forts along the rivers that were the only reliable channels of communication. This competitive fort-building anticipated by several years the renewal of hostilities in Europe. Each nation, seeking to establish by prior possession its right to the hinterland, searched for the perfect place for ambuscade, the ideal spot for prolonged defence. The ill-defined borders rang to the clash of arms as tiny regular garrisons, with colonial augmentations, strove for mastery with the limited means at their disposal.

With each formal declaration of war (there were many during the 18th century) the garrisons were increased and in 1755 a typical British reinforcement of 1,000 men under Major-General Edward Braddock arrived in the British part of the New World in anticipation of a renewal of war. Braddock's instructions directed him to prepare the way for an invasion of Canada by capturing strategically important French forts which could serve as bases. He was to bring his two under-strength regiments up to establishment by local recruitment.

By June 1755, a force of 2,000 was ready. The task was the capture of Fort Duquesne, a French post on the Ohio River. Most of the soldiers in the column were red-coated British regulars, but there were also several hundred blue-coated colonial militiamen under a Virginian gentleman named George Washington.

The advance was slow and methodical. The French had ample warning of the approach of the Anglo-American column. A Canadian historian, G. F. G. Stanley, has described what it must have looked like:

> The road to the fort narrowed as it rose from the river; both sides were crowded with heavy, dark forests which provided ample cover for the French and Indians but which hampered the movements of the regulars, trained to manoeuvre in the European manner in the open field.

Along it came the little army, in European tactical formation. Guides led the way, followed by flanking parties watching each side from the narrow track. Drums beat a marching pace, banners flew, officers chatted as they rode along. Behind the troops, a huge wagon-train of supplies lumbered along towed by oxen. Then, without warning, a force sent out from the fort as an ambuscade blundered into

15

the head of the column. On the narrow road, there could be no proper deployment. One British gun was wheeled into position and got off a charge of grape, but the French and Indians circled through the woods and attacked from the flanks. In Stanley's words, 'Within a few minutes the English and Americans had lost all cohesion and become a muddled, confused, bewildered mass. The European drill books of the day provided no easy answer to the problem of bringing a company in double column of twos into line for firing.'

The British column broke and fled, leaving their dead behind them. Braddock received a mortal wound, but lived long enough to utter the optimistic words by which we remember him. The force lost 1,000 men, 500 horses and all its artillery and stores. The French lost 8 officers and men and 15 Indians.

It was this debacle that resulted directly in the formation of the 60th Regiment, called from the first 'The Royal Americans'. Lord Loudoun, Braddock's ineffectual successor, was named 'Colonel-in-Chief', four battalions were authorized, and a special Bill was passed through Parliament permitting the granting of commissions to foreigners settled in North America provided they were Protestants. The Regiment's official historian for the period, Lewis Butler, notes dryly that 'to emphasize that the Regiment would be chiefly employed in bush warfare, the uniforms were made devoid of lace—a step, even though but a short one, in the right direction'. After a short period as the 62nd of Foot, disbandments elsewhere resulted in its renumbering as the 60th, a designation it carried permanently thereafter.

It was one thing to lay down red coats for wear by the new Regiment (laced or unlaced), but quite another to make it wear the dress in war. Red coats were like targets in the forest. From the first, backwoods dress and backwoods tactics were mandatory. When campaigning was over, the splendour came out again, but while battle loomed the Royal Americans were forest creatures, like the enemy they sought to defeat.

'What specially distinguished the new regiment,' wrote Lewis Butler, 'was the fact that among the seniors were several who had either served in the French army, or were . . . fully acquainted with its system.' Butler pointed

Henry Bouquet was born in Switzerland in 1719 and joined the Swiss Guard of the Prince of Orange after service in northern Italy. In 1756 he was appointed first Commanding Officer of the 1st Bn., the 60th Royal American Regiment in North America. Under Bouquet the 1st Bn. were the first British Regular Unit to adopt light and inconspicuous clothing and equipment, single drill open formation and rapid movement.

out that British Army training of the time was based on Prussian ideas; the men were drilled as 'unreasoning machines'. The early Commanding Officers of the 60th, notably Lieutenant-Colonels Frederick Haldimand and Henri Bouquet, 'cultivated the intelligence of each individual member of the corps'.

Thus from the first a special ethos characterized the regimental community of the 60th, which would be reflected later in the formation in England of the Light Division. This special atmosphere must be remembered when studying the many clashes with England's enemies that occupied the regiment from the time of its formation. Its creation was in itself an innovation, its officers military free-thinkers. This sense of being in the lead in military thought has been continued in a remarkable way through the years.

During the whole period from 1755 to 1783 there were always at least two, and often four, battalions of the Regiment in action in North America. To attempt to describe the history of each one would be to submerge the reader with data. One can only deal with the highlights with so many contending for space. Briefly, the fighting of the period can be divided into two preoccupations: first, the successful effort to drive the French and Spanish out of the eastern part of North America, and, second, the unsuccessful attempt to defeat the rebellious colonies.

All four of the new battalions were tested in 1758. During that year General James Abercromby led new assaults against the French. At Ticonderoga and at Louisburg the new units demonstrated their worth, although only the latter action could be deemed a success. The Regiment's new techniques were established when, in November, the 1st Battalion erased Braddock's failure by taking the leading role in capturing Fort Duquesne. The elimination of this key French post did more than any other operation to open up the interior to English expansion.

18

The next two years saw control of North America pass finally to Britain. At Quebec in 1759 and at Montreal in 1760, the French and their Indian allies were defeated. All four battalions of the 60th participated in these actions and two of them, the 2nd and 3rd, earned praise from General Wolfe that resulted in the authorization of the regimental motto, 'Swift and Bold' ('Celer et Audax'). The 1st Battalion, under Bouquet, was then given the task of holding the French forts of the interior, little dreaming that peace had not yet come to North America.

In February 1763, the Treaty of Amiens confirmed Great Britain as supreme east of the Mississippi. No further attempts were made by France to regain her lost dominions, but her former allies, the Indian tribes, loosely described as Algonquins, were not enamoured of the idea

The Death of General Wolfe at the Siege of Quebec.

19

of English rule. Under Pontiac, a chief of the Ottawas, an uprising was organized.

When the storm broke an English fur-trader named Alexander Henry was in the outpost of Michilimackinac (hoping to capture the markets surrendered by the French) and recorded one of the few eye-witness accounts of the terrifying experience. The garrison, which numbered only thirty-five, was asked to view a game of lacrosse staged by the local Indians, who were camped outside. At a hidden signal, the ball was tossed over the stockade into the fort and the Indians ran in after it. Tomahawks and knives were then suddenly produced and the garrison was quickly overwhelmed. Henry managed to escape, but not before witnessing appalling scenes of torture as the Indians wreaked vengeance on the English soldiers who had defeated their former French allies.

Incidents like this were repeated throughout the interior. The borders of Pennsylvania, Maryland and Virginia once more ran red with settlers' blood and smoked with burning farms. Only the largest forts, notably Detroit, were able to hold out. Relieving columns were soon organized, however, and the most successful of these was the one commanded by Henri Bouquet. He had tried to warn Jeffery Amherst, the somewhat pig-headed Commander-in-Chief, that the new parsimonious policies with the Indians, coming so soon after the prodigality of the French, would cause unrest. But Amherst (who had become Colonel-in-Chief of the 60th) thought he knew better. Now, with the border in flames, Bouquet's warnings were remembered and he was sent to command one of the columns ordered to suppress the uprising.

Amherst had few troops to cope with the situation; with the defeat of the French, many regiments had been withdrawn from North America and two battalions of the 60th (the 3rd and 4th) had been disbanded. It has been recorded that he made the suggestion that in some manner the

Indian tribes should be infected with smallpox in order to reduce the size of his problem. This man later became the Commander-in-Chief of the British Army!

Bouquet's force, when it mustered for the advance, numbered about 550 men, 150 of whom were Royal Americans, versed in forest fighting and dressed in buckskin, with two under-strength and disease-ridden Highland regiments, the 42nd and the 77th, to help. Bouquet headed towards Fort Detroit, a march of many hundreds of miles through Indian-infested frontier country.

On the way, his role was complicated by the necessity of succouring refugees from burning hamlets and replenishing the supplies of beleaguered ones. Nevertheless, he made steady progress, for he and his men had profited by previous encounters in the wilderness. On August 4 he began, as a first step, a march designed to relieve the garrison at Fort Duquesne, now named Fort Pitt. He had marched seventeen miles through the wilderness when his vanguard was fired on from the forest; he had come up with the insurgent Indians. The ensuing battle, which Bouquet and his men won with great dash, turned the scale in the forest operations. Recoiling on his wagon-train, which he had posted on high ground with a field of fire, he formed a defensive perimeter and invited attack.

Seven hours of savage fighting followed. Each attack was beaten off. Nightfall brought a halt, but Bouquet had lost 60 men of his force, and was out of water. At dawn the fight was renewed and Butler has visualized what it must have been like:

> Approaching under cover of the trees, the savages opened fire simultaneously from every side. Nearer and nearer they came—the perfection of skirmishers—making a beautiful example of a mode of attack a century and a half in advance of its age.

Bouquet's men were not so lost in admiration that they forgot their duty. In his report to Amherst, Bouquet wrote,

21

after telling of his losses, of 'my admiration for the cool and steady behaviour of the troops who did not fire a shot without orders, and drove the enemy from their posts with fixed bayonets'.

Nevertheless, some new factor was necessary if the force was to survive; with each charge it got smaller, and thirst was a major misery. With every counter-attack, the Indians melted into the forest and it seemed impossible to get him into the open. Bouquet, measuring the frenzy of his foe, decided to try a feigned withdrawal. He ordered two companies of the Royal Americans to pull back and take up concealed positions in the rear. The ruse worked, and the Indians rushed into the trap, to be assailed by a sudden weight of fire from the flanks, followed by a bayonet charge. Their attack withered away, and as they retired they were fired on from the flanks of the circle they had penetrated; the retirement became a rout. This operation, named Bushy Run after a nearby stream, proved conclusively, if proof were needed, that the 60th had heeded Braddock's last words and had 'learned better'. As Bouquet resumed his march towards Fort Pitt the surviving Indians could do no more than harass the determined column, which wintered at the fort on the Ohio, having successfully traversed 324 miles of hostile country.

In the summer of 1763 the Indians began to tire of besieging forts. It dawned on them that their former allies, the French, were not, after all, coming to their help. One by one the tribes slipped away to their regular hunting grounds and other British columns came to finish the work of Bouquet and his little army. By 1765 the Great Lakes and the Ohio were reasonably quiet again. Bouquet was promoted to Brigadier-General, but died soon after.

This imaginative Swiss has become a special figure in the history of the 60th. Reading the annals of the period, one is struck by the admiration he inspired. One ardent supporter goes so far as to suggest that had he lived,

Fort Loudoun 27ᵗʰ August 1764

Sir

I have the honor to transmit to you a
Letter from Colonel Bradstreet, who acquaints me
that he has granted Peace to all the Indians
living between Lake Erie and the Ohio: but
as no Satisfaction is insisted on: I hope the
General will not confirm it, and that I shall
not be a Witness to a Transaction which
would fix an Indelible Stain upon the Nation.

I therefore take no notice of that pretended
Peace, and proceed forthwith on the Expedition
fully determined to treat as Enemies any
Delawares or Shawanese I shall find in my
Way, till I receive contrary orders from the
General.

I have the honor to be with great Respect

Sir

Your most obedient
and most Humble Servant

Governor Penn   Henry Bouquet

*A letter from Henry Bouquet to Governor Penn announcing his intention
to ignore Colonel Bradstreet's Peace Treaty with the Indians.*

23

Britain might not have lost the American colonies. But this assumes that Bouquet would have sought Britain's side in the rebellion. George Washington, himself an imaginative campaigner, had to make this choice and the temptation of men like him to side with the indignant colonists must have been powerful. In fact, the British government had to face up to just such a possibility from its splendid new Royal American Regiment, when, within a few years, English loyalties were being tested in the New World.

Chapter 2

Oh, wherefore come ye forth in triumph from the north,
With your hands and your feet and your raiment all red?

MACAULAY

WITH THE Royal American Regiment firmly established as a distinguished, if eccentric, unit of Britain's regular army, its place in history seemed assured. But the regimental historian has described the ominous clouds that lay on the horizon for any unit raised in North America in the late 18th century.

> As fate willed, it was through the action of two officers of the Royal Americans that the strongest links binding the colonies to the mother country were broken. At Montreal, Amherst had destroyed the French power on the continent, and at the Muskingum (the final Indian surrender) Bouquet had forever removed the danger of the white man being exterminated by the red. With the disappearance of these perils the turbulent spirits among the colonists could, without fear of consequences, indulge their love of bickering with the mother country, and the attentive listener could already hear the growling of the storm destined to burst within ten short years.

For the time that remained, the Royal Americans did the usual garrison duty where danger lay. In 1762, the 3rd Battalion had participated in the capture of Martinique from the French, and Cuba from the Spanish, but these West Indian islands were used as pawns on the European chessboard. Within a year of their capture, Cuba was handed back to Spain and Martinique to France. At one time during this horse-trading, it was seriously proposed that Canada, too, be given back to France, in exchange for Guadeloupe.

The Regiment was unaware that it had only tasted the delights of West Indian fighting; much more lay ahead. But with the end of the Seven Years War it was reduced by the disbandment of the 3rd and 4th Battalions, while companies of the 1st and 2nd garrisoned forts in the Canadas and Western America. Here, British Commanders-in-Chief took little notice of the Regiment's experiments with campaign uniforms; the British army had worn red coats since Cromwell's time and there seemed no reason whatever for change.

As friction increased between England and her colonies, the Regiment's duties narrowed to those which seemed likely to remain loyal. The land that lay about the mouth of the St. Lawrence, Nova Scotia, which administered what was later to become New Brunswick and Prince Edward

Camp of the 60th Rifles at Kaministiquia River (circa 1770).

26

Island, showed no sign of disaffection, Lower Canada had accepted British rule, and Upper Canada was too remote and poor to be a factor. The Regiment was stationed at Montreal and Halifax, and, detachment by detachment, in the British West Indies.

It is difficult today to realize how deeply men's emotions were stirred by the American disaffections of the 1770s. The lack of good-will on both sides and the blunderings of an uncomprehending British government left deep scars on the characters of the participants. The issues that precipitated the struggle were complex; great patience was essential. It was lacking on both sides. Individual families were split by the dispute, and if George Washington could be called a traitor to his country by one side and a patriot by the other, there were many like him. Even old Jeffrey Amherst refused to have anything to do with any attempt to win back the colonies by force.

A regiment like the Royal Americans, therefore, simply could not be put in the position of having to fight colonists. The 1st and 2nd Battalions remained for the most part in the West Indies, and when new units were required, they were raised at home. The 3rd and 4th Battalions once more appeared on Orders of Battle and were dispatched from England to Florida, where, by 1777, the bulk of the British forces had withdrawn in hope of support from descendants of cavaliers who lived in Georgia and the Carolinas. The defence of Savannah, Georgia, was the outstanding Royal American achievement of this period, and the man responsible, Major-General Augustin Prevost, comes down to us as a towering figure in the 60th pantheon.

The operations that preceded the siege, conducted in the swamps and forests of the region, have a splendid cut-and-thrust quality to them, as columns pursued each other, captured and lost wilderness settlements, carried out ambuscades and generally had a wild and woolly time. The need was for speed, and it would appear that here too the

27

60th were flexible. The facts are meagre and the documentation (what exists of it) confusing, but it would appear that local planters provided horses for a corps of 'Rangers' made up largely of 60th volunteers, who could be termed the first 'mounted infantry'. They were led by Marc Prevost, a brother of the General, and proved a match for the best that could be sent against them.

As the weight of Revolutionary armies built up against him, General Prevost fell back on Savannah, a prosperous southern town on the Atlantic coast. In September 1779, he was attacked from the sea by a French fleet carrying 6,000 soldiers, and an American force from the interior of 4,000. Prevost successfully saw them off, after a series of furious but futile attacks, with a garrison of less than 4,000, many of them unfit for duty. In the end, after a siege of nearly a month, the French fleet withdrew, fearing the arrival of British ships, and the Americans retired into Carolina, leaving Georgia in British hands.

Less fortunate were those detachments of the Regiment dispersed in penny packets throughout the Caribbean and elsewhere in the Deep South. As the war raged back and forth through the fever-lands, names like Fort San Juan, Pensacola, New Orleans, Baton Rouge and Mobile survive in the history books, although few of the British garrisons did so for long. When not under attack by several nations (even Holland re-entered the contest briefly in 1780), the luckless remnants of British power in the south died like flies of malaria, yellow fever, and dysentery.

Finally, after Yorktown, it was over. New York held out long enough to receive the survivors of the 3rd and 4th Battalions, and then the Peace of Versailles, in 1783, confirmed the undoubted fact that the rebellious colonies had achieved independence. Canada and Nova Scotia remained loyal and for some years thereafter the Royal Americans were restricted to garrison duty in the northern bastions of British influence. Within three years the whole

The storming of Fort San Juan, on the river St. John which is the outlet of Lake Nicaragua into the Gulf of Mexico (1780).

Regiment was stationed in British North America, the 1st in Halifax, the 2nd in Montreal, the 3rd and 4th having, as usual, been disbanded after the fighting.

By 1793 and the outbreak of war with Republican France, the 3rd and 4th had been reactivated and had gone through more years of misery in the West Indies. Britain, as usual, had no army to speak of with which to intervene on the continent, but her navy could influence events abroad. Once more the dreary list of tropical islands lost and won crops up in the accounts of gallantry and fortitude as Martinique came again and San Domingo and finally, as the tempo increased, Tobago. This small action stands

29

out as a classic example of what the troops were asked to accomplish. The official regimental historian has the story:

> On April 12, 1793, the 4th Battalion of the 60th, 321 all ranks, under Major William Gordon, with two companies of the 9th Regiment, 97 strong, and 50 gunners, sailed from Barbadoes . . .

This force, of less than 500, was charged with capturing a defended island from the French which had not been reconnoitred since it had last been occupied by the British, thirty years before. Arriving on April 14, the squadron protecting the landing force anchored in the harbour and put the tiny army ashore. The British commander, one General Cuyler, demanded instant surrender from the fort. When this was 'treated with contumely' he sat down to consider the situation.

Major Gordon, the commander of the 60th, volunteered to lead a silent night attack, and Cuyler consented. In the approach to the fort, part of the force became separated in the darkness, and this fortunate mistake resulted in an assault from two directions, dividing the attention of the garrison. Thus, while half his troops distracted the defenders from one side, Gordon with the rest tumbled into the moat around the defences. There they found themselves up against a high wall the existence of which they had not been aware.

> Halting his men for a minute's rest, the Major cried, 'God save the King: follow me' and was answered by three hearty cheers. Up the rampart he clambered, followed by a corporal; the pair pulled up the colours and about a dozen men with the aid of their firelocks. The first four were shot down, but others followed . . . When the party was complete it charged over the parapet and drove the enemy from his guns without firing a shot. Monsieur Montel, the Governor, then surrendered.

It will be noticed, in this account, that the 60th had, for the moment, lost its cunning ways of war, together with its rifles. It had not yet penetrated the official mind that techniques learned in the forest could have any bearing on events elsewhere. The gallantry remained, and the inspiration, together with a glorious 'take a chance' attitude, but the skills of open order fighting had been laid aside, along with 'battledress'.

More 'island hopping' in the Caribbean followed the capture of Tobago. Nearly all the attacks involved parties of the 60th. By this time *ad hoc* regiments were being made up from the survivors of previous assaults. The fortunes of individual companies of the Regiment were submerged in the confusion of attack and counter-attack. Only fragmentary and inaccurate copies of the Army List and old men's tales survive to record actions which, planned in Whitehall, took little account of actual conditions.

As the 18th century drew to a close and England began to see that the latest war with France might last a long time, the 60th underwent a dramatic change. The speed with which Republican France had demolished the carefully drilled armies of Austria and Prussia forced a re-examination of the structure of the British Army and the progressive thought of many 60th officers was reflected at long last in drastic changes. In December 1797, a fifth battalion was added to the Regiment, to be equipped as a 'rifle corps' and dressed in green.

Colonel Bouquet, the 'free thinker' of the Indian wars, had anticipated this kind of change by many years. His reflections on dress, long resisted as heresy by the authorities, seem like elementary common-sense today:

> The clothing of a soldier for the campaign should consist of a short jacket of brown cloth, a strong tanned shirt, short trowsers, leggings, mocassins, a sailor's hat, a knapsack for provisions and an oiled surtout against the rain.

This dress had worked in North America. It was a different matter in Europe. There, commanders in the field relied on the colour of uniforms as a quick means of

31

identification; lacking other communications, there was no better way of telling friend from foe. On battlefields obscured by the billowing smoke from musket and cannon, a sudden glimpse of blue, a flash of red, saved more than one army. Green was as far as the authorities were prepared to go in the direction of camouflage.

Lord Amherst died as the 5th Battalion was being formed and H.R.H. Prince Frederick, Duke of York, who loved playing at soldiers, was made Colonel-in-Chief of the 60th. In no time at all he had himself painted in the full dress of the new Battalion. When one considers that the full dress of the day differed in only slight degree from that worn on the battlefield, one can only wonder at the evolution of what was meant to be an inconspicuous garment for skirmishers.

Based on a light cavalry pattern, the officer's jacket was green, with scarlet facings, rows of black lace (frogging),

His Royal Highness the Duke of York—dressed to kill!

32

and three rows of silver buttons. There was a crimson sash about the waist and blue-grey trousers. With full dress, green breeches and hessian boots were worn instead of trousers. As if this were not enough, a black leather pouch-belt was also worn over the shoulder and across the body to the waist, complete with a silver plate, whistle and chain. A curious-looking cocked hat, with a large feather, completed the picture. The men wore a green jacket with red edging, a white waistcoat, blue breeches, black gaiters and a black shako. From the first, all ranks cultivated moustaches, a departure from previous infantry regulations. This was a far cry from Bouquet's ideal campaigning dress, but it did set the 60th apart from infantry of the line, and it did provide some protective colouring.

How much this uniform was the Duke of York's conception, and how much the new Commanding Officer's, is conjectural. Lieutenant-Colonel Baron Francis de Rothenburg, whose ideas on how to train men have given him a special place among the Regiment's immortals, must certainly have been consulted. De Rothenburg was one of those international soldiers who had served cheerfully in several armies and knew no other career. The Revolution had driven him from France, but his military sympathies lay where battle beckoned. The author of a textbook on the training of riflemen and light infantry, he soon made his presence felt in the British Army; before long the new Battalion of the 60th resembled in many particulars the German 'Jäger' units, troops trained to be a commander's 'eyes' on the battlefield. The idea caught on and, at the same time that the 5th Battalion was made a rifle battalion, the other four were given a rifle company each.

De Rothenburg's coming to the 60th was a most fortunate event, for his theories were picked up by men like Sir John Moore and eventually spread throughout the army. In addition to forward-looking tactical concepts, that took notice of new inventions like the rifle, de Rothenburg's method included extensions of Bouquet's teachings on man-management. Flogging was all but abolished under him, officers were taught to know their men and to treat them as reasoning humans, cleanliness and personal pride were fostered and dignity was restored to the rank and file. As a result, of course, the Battalion's performance was greatly improved and officers who could justify barbaric cruelties to the men on various grounds, ranging from stupidity to ingrained sloth, were pleased to have the 60th beside, or in front of, them when battle loomed.

All the battalions of the Regiment had an international flavour in the early years of its history. Royalist emigrés from France, mercenaries from the German states, Polish adventurers, all were happily gathered in by the Regiment's recruiting officers. Freed as they were by the regulations that had been devised to organize the corps in the beginning, they were not restricted to enlisting Englishmen. But this had one unhappy result: the 60th spent an inordinate length of time abroad, much of it in the fever-ridden West Indies. When a sixth battalion was organized in 1799, the authorities lost no time in dispatching it to join the four others stationed there. The 6th Battalion wore green, too, but with white breeches to distinguish it from the 5th. It is doubtful if any dress distinction mattered after a while in the battles for islands that soon absorbed it.

The new century—which brought brief hope that the Peace of Amiens would end hostilities—soon disillusioned the optimistic when Anglo-French hostility flared again. Each side once more sought continental alliances, which, when arranged, brought prompt reaction in the islands. After the Peace of Amiens, Martinique, Tobago, Santa Lucia and Demerara were given back to France. When war broke out again, they all had to be recaptured. When Holland entered the war, its colony, Surinam (Dutch Guiana), had also to be attacked. When Denmark came in, the 'Saints' (St. Croix, St. Thomas, and St. John's) were immediate targets.

From their bases on Barbados and Jamaica the battalions of the 60th participated in most of these expeditions. The survivors of previous campaigns knew Martinique, for example, as well as they knew their 'home' islands. The regimental historian calls these years in the West Indies 'dark days' and it is doubtful if the prints published for home consumption that showed victorious attacks by smartly dressed red and green clad troops bore much resemblance to the spent, tattered men who actually did the work.

As the war continued, recruits were harder to find. Many of the reinforcements were criminals, deserters from enemy armies, even French prisoners-of-war. These men must have taxed the enthusiasm of officers imbued with the regimental tradition of a reasonable discipline. A battalion that became reduced to non-effective strength by battle or disease left its remaining strength with another, more recently arrived unit, and sailed back to England to re-build. In 1808, this happened to the 2nd Battalion of the 60th.

After visits to Jersey (a prisoner-of-war camp) and Plymouth, it unexpectedly sailed for Spain in the Division commanded by Sir David Baird. It was available, so it was used. On November 3, it landed at Corunna, to be the first battalion of the 60th to fight in what has become known as the Peninsular campaign. The 2nd did not advance with Baird's column; it was left to garrison the port, perhaps because of the nationality of its rank and file. It participated with honour in the last rearguard actions, embarked with the rest of the army, recruited up to strength again in England, and sailed for Barbados in November 1809. It had been away from the Indies for about a year.

It had barely arrived when its flank companies were grouped with the grenadier companies of the 4th Battalion and sent off to attack Guadeloupe. The operation was successful, but the quality of the new recruits must have left something to be desired, for the Commander-in-Chief got off a stinging rebuke to those in authority in England: 'I repeat my request that certain corps in this army be no longer loaded with men polluted by civil crimes, congregated with French prisoners and deserters.'

If the 'authorities' were unduly disturbed by this censure there is no record of it and the practice of enlisting foreign troops into the 60th continued when such troops were available.

Meanwhile, history was waiting for the 5th Battalion, which, in 1808, had been putting down restless natives in Ireland. In June, it was 'warned for active service' as a part of a 9,000-man force commanded by 39-year-old Lieutenant-General Sir Arthur Wellesley. The Peninsular campaign was about to be reopened in earnest.

Chapter 3

The Commander of the Forces recommends the Companies of the 5th Battalion of the 60th Regiment . . . to the General Officers commanding the Brigades of Infantry to which they are attached. They will find them to be most useful, active and brave troops . . .
                                    SIR ARTHUR WELLESLEY, 1809

THE 5TH BATTALION that set off for Spain in Wellesley's army was more German than English; the muster rolls of its officers read like an invitation list to a levee at Potsdam. These were the international soldiers, the careerists in uniform. They flocked to join a British army that owed allegiance to England's Hanoverian Kings. Volunteer units that were under-strength, like Hompesch's Light Infantry, Lowenstein's Chasseurs and The Royal Foreigners, mustered gladly into the 60th to fight the French. They were well-trained, good shots with the rifle, and there was no reason to doubt their loyalty.

Napoleon had put his brother, Joseph, on the throne of Spain, setting off a popular uprising that had tempted Britain into sending aid in the shape of an expeditionary force. The only large contingent available was the 9,000-man garrison at Cork, which included the 5th Battalion. Major W. G. Davy commanded; de Rothenburg had just been promoted to Brigadier-General. On July 12, 1808 the convoy sailed and on August 1 the 5th Battalion was the first unit ashore at Mondego Bay some hundred miles north of Lisbon.

The actions that followed, as Wellesley marched along the coastal road towards the Portuguese capital, were neat, well-fought and effective. For the first of these encounters,

Rolica, the 5th Battalion was joined by four companies of the 95th (the Rifle Brigade), to form a Light Brigade. The unit was charged with producing advanced guards on the march and skirmishers on the flanks in battle. In the advance to Lisbon, the Light Brigade led the way, about one day's march ahead of the main body. The 95th were in the van when the first brush with the French occurred at the village of Obidos. The enemy evacuated at speed. The Rifle Brigade could thus claim that it had fired the first shots of the Peninsular campaign. A series of turning movements followed, culminating in an attack on the French force near Rolica. The 60th were deeply involved on the right, climbing steep hills under fire and driving the French before them. Wellesley, hearing that his newly-appointed superior, Sir Harry Burrard, was about to land at Mondego Bay with reinforcements, took up a covering position about Vimiero. By this time the 60th had been affected by a battlefield reorganization, Wellesley having issued an order that they should supply at least one company and sometimes more to each brigade to act as advanced guards and skirmishers. This disrupted the battalion organization and no 'regimental' battles were thereafter fought by the 5th, but it did mean that men of the 60th were present at almost every fight.

On August 21, 1808 they were the first to feel the weight of the sudden attack launched on the Vimiero position by General Junot, who was in command at Lisbon. It was a rash thing for the French general to do, for Wellesley out-numbered him. Junot's over-confidence resulted in his decisive defeat and the remnants of his force streamed back in the direction of Lisbon. Burrard forbade Wellesley to pursue; these were still the days of generalship on the battlefield, and armies were small enough to command in person. But Vimiero was decisive, not least because it was here that Wellesley's tactics were established. Siting his battle-line on reverse slopes, he forced the French to deploy with his skirmishers, and then, when the attackers were exhausted by the effort, his fresh line fired volley after volley into the disorganized French columns.

The 60th and the 95th performed their allotted role, in front of the defenders, picking off the leaders, disrupting the advance. Colonel Charles Leslie, writing years later in the *Aberdeen Free Press*, described a battlefield incident at Vimiero that illustrates vividly the skill with the rifle that the 60th commanded:

> . . . the 60th riflemen, who were all German, showed . . . dexterity in the use of their arms. General Fane (commanding one of the brigades on the left flank), observing one of these men successfully hit one of the French officers . . . exclaimed in the excitement of the moment, 'Well done, my fine fellow! I will give you half a doubloon for every other one you bring down.' The man eagerly loaded again, fired and hit another, then, looking at the General, he said gravely, 'By God, I vill make my vortune.'

Rifleman Harris of the 95th was at Vimiero, and recorded his recollection of 60th officers. He had just killed a French soldier who had taken two unsuccessful shots at him, and was looking over the body for plunder, when an officer of the 60th approached. Harris explained that he could not find where the Frenchman had hidden his hoard. The officer said, 'You knocked him over, my man, in good style and deserve something for the shot.' Then he showed Harris where the French usually hid their money. Harris ripped open the dead man's jacket lining, where he found a heavy purse just as the officer had said. Then assembly was sounded. Harris thanked the officer for his courtesy, saluted and returned to his own lines.

These tales take some understanding these days. In fact, battlefield loot was about all a soldier could look forward to in 1808, and it was a powerful incentive. What is understandable about the stories is the mutual respect that existed between regimental officers and their men. There were times when the lust for loot broke this down, and the horrific scenes that stain the memory of the retreat to Corunna, or the sack of Badajos, resulted. Then the absolute power to punish was used to restore order. In the main, however, the troops in the Peninsula were well commanded, by officers who knew their men. There was much gallantry—even chivalry—shown by both sides on the battlefield. It was the sieges of cities that drove men mad; they were the least successful of Wellington's operations, the casualties were always heavy, and the orgies that followed all too many of them are understandable, if unforgivable.

With Vimiero a clear-cut victory, and the French in full retreat, Wellesley's reinforced army appeared to have an open road before it, but Burrard remained cautious, and within a matter of days another senior officer, Sir Hew Dalrymple, arrived to command. The result was a steady deterioration of the administrative apparatus and a remarkable battlefield agreement that permitted the French to evacuate Lisbon under arms and return to France in British ships. Wellesley soon had enough of it and went back to Ireland, after he, Dalrymple and Burrard had been ordered home to explain their lack of result; Sir John Moore took over. The 5th Battalion did not march with his army; its Commanding Officer, Major Davy, had taken a step which landed him and his battalion in serious trouble.

Briefly, Davy asked for, and received, permission to enlist French prisoners-of-war. There were many Germans serving in the French army and, as we have seen, there was many a precedent in the Regiment's history for the move. Over 100 men of the French army were persuaded to change their uniforms and their allegiance. Unfortunately, when near their former friends, they tended to return to them and, since Moore was soon fighting a rearguard action against an enemy that outnumbered him three to one, he could not take a chance on the elements of the 5th Battalion that had these uncertain soldiers. As a result, the 5th Battalion was ordered back to Portugal, missing, in the process, the retreat to Corunna and the subsequent return to England. This unpleasant turn of events had one unexpected result; the battalion served in the Peninsula from beginning to end of the campaign.

The 5th Battalion, once concentrated again as a unit, soon put its affairs in order, divesting itself of the untrustworthy, and re-equipping its tattered companies. In April 1809, Sir Arthur Wellesley, restored to the command, returned to Portugal to begin a campaign that was to go down in history as one of the great feats of British arms.

Wellesley wasted no time in Lisbon. In five days he had completed his administrative arrangements, once more decentralized his Rifle companies among the brigades, organized his 25,000 British troops into four divisions, collected together some 16,000 Portuguese troops, and begun to march north against Marshal Soult, who was camped about the town of Oporto. Driving the French rearguards across the Douro, he forced the river (there is reason to believe that No. 5 Company of the 5th Battalion was the first to cross) and sent Soult flying into Spain without a battle. Wellesley had thus cleared Portugal in nine days, at a cost of about 500 casualties. Moore had been amply revenged.

The only other French force in the western part of the Peninsula was Marshal Victor's, at Merida, just east of the Portuguese border. Wellesley set off to attack him but Victor retreated from a district he had exhausted of supplies, and in which he was threatened with Spanish troops and guerrillas. Nevertheless, Victor was still an attractive target and Wellesley went after him, aided by about 33,000 Spaniards.

By mid-July, Victor had taken up a position about the

town of Talavera with his left resting on the River Tagus and his right on a thickly wooded hill. He had only 22,000 men and his carelessly chosen position invited attack by the superior Anglo-Spanish force. But, as Wellesley was to find out, it was one thing to help the Spanish, but quite another thing to get them to help in return. While the Spanish general delayed, Victor withdrew and the chance was lost. Then the Spanish army went marching off on a wild goose chase. Wellesley was left on his own with 22,000 men on half rations and the knowledge that King Joseph, with an army of 46,000, was marching to join Victor.

On July 27, the Spaniards returned and, with Wellesley, took up a strong position east of Talavera, there to await attack. The Spaniards, whom one historian, W. H. Maxwell, has called a 'useless mob', were placed on the right on top of a slope so broken that it would have been folly to attack it. The blow, when it came, fell entirely on the British line.

The first brush with the enemy occurred when the 3rd Division, which was thrown out in front to protect the occupation of the position, was attacked by three columns of French troops hurrying towards the battlefield. The unexpectedness of the assault caught several units off balance and they became disorganized and broke before the assaulting French. This left the skirmishing line to be held by some 250 men of the 60th and the whole of the 45th Regiment. Falling back slowly, in good order, firing and withdrawing, they gave precious time for the line behind them to re-form, and may have prevented the capture of Wellesley, who was reconnoitring nearby. Their 'gallantry, steadiness and discipline' were commented on in the Commander-in-Chief's next General Order. The 60th had recovered from the infusion of poor material after Vimiero.

During the evening the French closed up to the British position and Victor tried a night attack on the left, which was beaten back. At dawn on the 28th, he launched a full-scale effort, preceded by an intense bombardment. The French came on, as was their custom, in column, but the musketry of the British line blew away the heads of each one and flank fire from the 60th, who had as usual fallen back to each side of the attack, helped to disorganize the assault. The attackers withdrew, leaving 1,300 casualties behind them. Victor was determined to try again, and in spite of the protests of his colleagues (King Joseph and Marshal Jourdan had joined him) he launched a fresh assault at 2 p.m., this time against the British centre.

This was no more successful than the previous attempts. Wellesley and his staff occupied a hill called Cerro de Medellin, which overlooked the whole battlefield, and there was ample time for him to adjust the British dispositions to meet the French attack. The fighting was fierce and prolonged, but the British line held. The broken French regiments streamed back to their starting point where a raging Victor, who wanted to try yet again, was persuaded of his folly and ordered a general retreat. The next morning found him gone, having suffered 7,268 casualties. The British loss was 5,365. Portugal was safe for a time and Wellesley became Viscount Wellington as a reward for Talavera.

His first task was to shake his army loose from dependence on the Spanish army; they had promised much and produced little. To do this he needed supply trains, stocks of food and ammunition and a plan within the capacity of the British and Portuguese troops at his disposal. It took six months to do all this, and no amount of pressure from England or from Spain would hurry him. In the end his stubborn stand was amply justified by his successes.

Wellington's technique, when he saw a chance to strike at the French, was to tempt them to battle, form up on carefully selected ground, and then invite attack. To do this he had to find ground that the French would be forced to attack, that was at the same time suitable for his concept of defence. Time after time the technique worked, for the French could not stand the idea of having this persistent enemy at large in Spain, and the Napoleonic method was always to attack. But from the time that Wellington arrived, there was no Napoleon to make the French method work; the great man was busy elsewhere and left Spain to his marshals.

There were to be four more years of campaigning in the Peninsula, years of marching, counter-marching, siege and battle. The 60th, due to their skirmishing and advanced guard role, participated in almost all the activity, and earned no less than fifteen battle honours. It is fortunate that Wellington's methods, dictated by his slender re-sources, became stylized, for if one describes one action in the Peninsula, like Talavera, the others that followed become recognizable.

Masséna was the next marshal to have a try at evicting the British from the Peninsula and his operations in Spain and Portugal were the highlights of 1810. Marching into Portugal with a force of 65,000 men and 50 guns, he soon found himself in the arid country which the Portuguese and Wellington had turned into a desert. At Busaco, on September 27, Wellington found a favourable defensive position across the route of Masséna's advance, and a repetition of Talavera followed. His main line concealed by the crest of a high hill, his front protected by what one French observer called 'black specks at equal intervals . . . whose short rifles were so murderous', the battle began at dawn, and was over by noon. The mixed force of British and Portuguese suffered 1,250 casualties, the French lost nearly 5,000.

Next day, Masséna began a turning movement against the British force and Wellington withdrew behind his recently constructed Lines of Torres Vedras. Masséna followed, was appalled by the lines, which he did not know existed, lingered stubbornly until his rations gave out and then fell back, covered by a large rearguard under Marshal Ney.

In April 1811, Wellington laid siege to the town of Almeida, garrisoned by 1,500 of the enemy. His purpose was not to take the place, which had little that was worth fighting for, but to force Masséna into a battle for it. Masséna swallowed the bait and Wellington chose a likely defensive position near Fuentes d'Onor. The ensuing battle lasted two days and went according to British plans. The 5th Battalion distinguished itself throughout. The Commanding Officer, Lieutenant-Colonel Williams, was seriously wounded during the first day, when the under-strength companies of the 60th held, almost alone, a vital portion of the line about the village of Fuentes d'Onor itself. Most of the rifle companies had a strength of less than fifty men. After losing twice as many men as the defenders, Masséna withdrew again to Ciudad Rodrigo. His skill as a general had been gravely diminished by Wellington's rough handling, and the Emperor replaced him with his youngest marshal, Marmont, to see what he could do with the small but scratchy British force which persisted in defying the hitherto undefeated armies of France.

The business of investing walled towns was continued by both sides throughout the rest of the year. On May 16, 1811, Hill's Corps, commanded temporarily by Beresford, stood off an attempt by Soult to break through to Badajos and, in spite of a badly mismanaged battle, inflicted more casualties than it received. The 5th Battalion suffered less than most in this action, as, from their covered positions, they swept the enemy flanks with aimed fire. This battle of Albuera, named after the village around which it was fought, was duly added to the lengthening list of 60th battle honours.

Throughout 1811, Wellington manœuvred against

three French armies. His aim of keeping them out of Portugal was achieved and the unsettled state of the country prevented them from concentrating long enough to overpower him with numbers. Whenever they did attempt to combine he slipped away. The marching and countermarching that all this entailed was hard on the troops, but by the end of the year they had learned to live with it. Such tactics, however, did not win campaigns. They could at best keep the French on the move, with the ever-present possibility that one of the three forces would make a mistake.

Wellington, who unlike Napoleon waiting to enter Russia had few weather problems, struck early in January. His aim was the reduction of the fortress town of Ciudad Rodrigo, which had a garrison of 2,000. The outer redoubts were captured by January 15, and by the 19th two breaches had been made in the walls. A night attack followed, and after bitter fighting, which cost the British 500 casualties, the town was carried and the garrison surrendered. Unfortunately, the attractions of a captured town were too much for the troops and much looting and debauchery followed.

Now it was the turn of Badajos, with its larger garrison. Without these two places in British hands Wellington's ultimate aim, an advance on Madrid, could not be attempted, for in French hands they blocked his line of communication with Portugal. Badajos was a much tougher nut to crack; its commander was a man of enterprise, its garrison twice as large as that at Ciudad Rodrigo. Further, the menace of Marmont's army was always there away to the north-east, to say nothing of Soult's to the south. The siege was begun on March 17, and it took three weeks to develop two breaches large enough to attack. It was the task of the 5th Battalion's unattached companies, reinforced, to cover the advance of the storming parties of the 3rd Division, whose attack was meant to be a mere diversion. But luck, determination and the presence of that re-

46

doubtable warrior General Picton worked a miracle. While the Riflemen took a toll of the defenders on the wall, ladders were hoisted at a weak point, and the leading elements of the 3rd Division flowed into the town.

It was just as well; the battle at the main breaches was going badly. Hundreds of bodies piled up as attack after attack failed to penetrate the stubborn defence. Then the word that the 3rd Division was in the town reached the French and the defence slackened. Within minutes the British were triumphant and the ugly scenes of Ciudad Rodrigo were re-enacted on a much worse scale. The British lost 5,000 men in the assault. Wellington was rewarded with an Earldom. The 60th chalked up another battle honour.

With the two frontier fortresses in British hands, Wellington could now turn his attention to Madrid, where King Joseph husbanded the French reserves and watched the fighting in the west with increasing nervousness. He had good reason. On June 9 Wellington began to march east, leaving General Hill's corps to watch Marmont and his Spanish allies to watch Soult.

Wellington's march to, and capture of, Salamanca prodded Marmont into an attempt to relieve it, and Wellington turned aside to do battle. Marmont was young and confident, and believed he had taken Wellington's measure. The manœuvring that followed was based on Marmont's belief that Wellington would never attack; his technique of defending chosen ground seemed to the French marshal to be his only way of fighting. This belief led to Marmont's undoing, for on June 22, while attempting to outflank the British (as usual drawn up on a reverse slope with the 5th Battalion skirmishing in front), he permitted one part of his column to drag behind some four miles. Wellington, watching from commanding ground, swiftly ordered an attack on the head of Marmont's sundered column, leaving the cavalry to hold off the lagging half. The sudden assault, so utterly unexpected, threw the French into confusion, which was added to by the wounding of Marmont. By nightfall the remnants were streaming away from the field in disorder. Marmont's army had ceased, for the moment, to exist.

With this shattering stroke Wellington had opened the way to Madrid; without Marmont, King Joseph could not defend his capital. He fled, and on August 12 Wellington entered the capital. So did the scattered companies of the 60th, but without the gallant Colonel Williams, who had received his sixth wound at Salamanca and returned to England, turning over the command to Major J. F. Fitzgerald.

The British did not linger in Madrid; there were still French armies roaming Spain. Clausel, who had succeeded Marmont, gathered together 20,000 men and marched to threaten Wellington's rear. Burgos was besieged, French columns marched to relieve the town before it could be taken, and the British withdrew. An order from France directed all the French forces to unite against the presumptuous British, and the long columns of red and blue began again to criss-cross the dun-coloured landscape of Spain, seeking a decision. By late autumn, King Joseph was back in his capital, and French armies were closing in on the weary British forces from three sides. But when it came to a decision, the French hesitated, and Wellington gained the Portuguese border with his army reduced by privation, but intact. The 5th Battalion was rather better off than most, although nearly 200 under-strength. The French dispersed to their areas of responsibility, their main preoccupations being the suppression of insurgents and the search for food.

As both sides in Spain paused to regroup, Napoleon, his pyrrhic victory at Moscow behind him, began the long march home. It was a time for action, and once again Wellington planned for a spring offensive.

The French were spread all over Spain in five armies each about 50,000 strong; misleading figures, for at least 30,000 were sick in hospitals. Against them, and more or less ready to march, were some 85,000 Spaniards in several semi-independent armies, and Wellington's army of about 65,000 men of whom 10,000 were Portuguese troops. This mixture of nationalities was reflected deeply in the 5th Battalion. A strength state dated April 25, 1813 shows that, of the officers, eighteen were British and twelve were foreign and all but one of the N.C.O.s and men were of foreign origin.

The end of France's domination of Europe could now be foreseen, but her armies refused to acknowledge it. The year 1813 saw them driven out of Spain and into France, but it was not easy. Napoleon seemed to recover his old flair and the Allies, who had thought to hurry him off his throne after the Russian disaster, found themselves defeated at Lutzen and Bautzen. It took the battle of Vitoria to arouse the Emperor's enemies to one last effort.

The campaign began in May, as Wellington, his army refreshed and reinforced, began to outflank the French armies to the north and east of him. Before long he had manœuvred them away from the coast, moved his port from Lisbon to Santander, on the Bay of Biscay, and forced his enemy to withdraw in the direction of the Pyrenees. King Joseph, burdened with a long and cumbersome train of loot-laden wagons and camp followers, decided to make a stand at Vitoria.

All the companies of the 5th Battalion saw heavy fighting in the battle that followed, but Colonel FitzGerald, commanding a force of Rifle and Light companies, made a decisive contribution. In an assault against the vital village of Arinez, his command held it, and forced the French, whose line had also been penetrated elsewhere, to pull back through Vitoria and take the road east to Pamplona. It was one of Wellington's few 'attack' battles and the retreat could quickly have become a rout, but the amount of booty strewn about the battlefield slowed the pursuit; regrettably, the Allied army paused as the troops were diverted to the masses of stolen treasure left behind by the French. It was a most effective, if costly, way of preventing further defeat. As it was, the French lost 150 guns and 7,000 men. But they were retiring on their supply line and they were still a cohesive force.

After Vitoria, Napoleon removed King Joseph's crown and sent Marshal Soult to command. Lord Wellington was promoted to the rank of Field-Marshal; his victory had prompted the Allies to try again in Germany.

There now remained the task of breaching the mountain ranges that separate Spain from France. This was no easy task; the passes could be held by few against many, as Roland had discovered at Roncesvalles. Further, a re-inforced Soult (all the French armies in Spain were now concentrated under his command, except for a few garrisons) decided on an offensive policy. Streaming down from the mountains, they attacked Wellington first, then Hill. This was playing Wellington's game, and Soult's army was soon fleeing back through the passes into France. Wellington might well have pursued, but the political situation in north-eastern Europe gave him pause and he contented himself with establishing good positions along the Pyrenees and besieging the last French garrison of any account, the seaport of San Sebastian. Soult tried to intervene, was driven off, and the port fell with heavy British casualties.

As October opened, Wellington was on the march again, and on the 7th forced his way across the Bidassoa, and on to French soil. There was to be much further fighting, and many casualties, before the campaign ended at Toulouse, but in D. J. Goodspeed's words 'the truth of the matter was that continued defeats had begun to take the heart out of the French Army'. The Nivelle was crossed, and then the Nive and, as Beresford and his Portuguese army began to march towards Bordeaux, Wellington headed north-east to Toulouse. Napoleon's abdication, on April 4, came six days before the final assault on that city. The war was over, and the last battle had been unnecessary.

In summing up, the enemy, surprisingly, has the most telling compliment on the activities of the 60th during the Peninsular War. Marshal Soult, in a letter to the Minister of War, wrote:

> There is in the English army a battalion of the 60th made up of ten companies (the regiment has six battalions, the other five are in America or the Indies). This battalion is never concentrated; it supplies one company to each infantry division in the army. *It is armed with carbines; the men are chosen for their marksmanship;* they perform the duties of scouts, and in action are expressly ordered to shoot the officers, especially the senior officers and generals. Thus it has been observed that whenever a superior officer goes to the front during an action, either to reconnoitre, or to direct his troops, or to stir up the battle, he is usually hit.
>
> This method of making war and injuring the enemy hurts us; our casualties in officers are so great that after two battles all are usually out of action. Yesterday, I saw battalions whose officers had been killed or wounded in the ratio of one officer to eight men; I also saw battalions which were reduced to two or three officers, although less than one sixth of their men had been put out of action.

It is an interesting commentary of the times that Soult should be so indignant; his upset was a survival from the age when an officer could stay a lance poised by a common soldier by crying 'I am a gentleman in coat armour!'. Napoleon had made war a serious business, involving nations, and not a variation of the hunting season. The thing was to win, and that meant using all the available skill. The skill of the 60th was becoming legendary.

Chapter 4

Good friends, sweet friends, let me not stir you up,
To such a sudden flood of mutiny.

SHAKESPEARE
Julius Caesar

WHILE THE 5th Battalion was upholding regimental tradition in the Peninsular War, the rest of the Regiment served as opportunity offered and grew as the need arose. A sixth battalion was raised in 1799 for service in the West Indies, but only one company was designated as a 'rifle company'. By 1813, however, the rifle 'idea' and the green uniform had gained general acceptance and when a seventh and eighth battalion were raised, one in Gibraltar and one in Lisbon, all wore green and all carried rifles.

There were no battalions of the 60th at Waterloo. After Napoleon's first abdication, the authorities found so many tasks for the Regiment around the world that none were in reach when the Hundred Days began. Many ex-60th officers were present, however, at Quatre Bras and later; the lists of commanders and staff of the period are heavy with Riflemen. But in the inevitable reductions of establishment that followed the final downfall of the Emperor, many went on half pay as no less than six battalions of the Regiment were disbanded. During this period, too, the Regiment parted with its foreign-born element, many representatives of which settled in Canada.

When the smoke of retrenchment cleared away, only the 2nd and 3rd Battalions remained, to be redesignated the 1st and 2nd. Even at that, the 60th were more fortunate

52

than the rest of the infantry, most of which became one-battalion regiments in the long peace that followed the Napoleonic wars. In fact, the term 'peace' at this period had more than one shade of meaning; there was usually a war going on somewhere on a modest scale. The regimental historian of the 60th, in heading the chapter from 1848 to 1895, uses the title 'Fourteen Minor Wars' and the 60th participated in most of them. They followed a familiar pattern: an outrage upon a British camp or garrison, a defiance of duly constituted authority, a relief column, a jolly good fight, a patched-up peace. An Empire always has these problems. The British were fortunate in having modern legions to keep the frontiers safe.

In this more leisurely atmosphere (an adjective the hard-marching troops would not have used) there was time to

Soldiers of the 60th dressed in Heavy marching order (circa 1830).

turn into regulations the loosely-held traditions that had come down the years with the Regiment. The marching pace was standardized at 140 to the minute, the special bayonet which the early rifle had demanded was now officially called a sword, the rifle was always carried at the trail or the 'carry' on the march (a relic of the Indian wars when a sloped musket caught in the undergrowth), the bugle whose calls had been the battle signals of a dispersed, skirmishing line appeared on cap badges, and the Maltese cross which the 5th Battalion had adopted as a badge

A native pillow belonging to King Cetywayo captured during the Zulu War (one of the fourteen minor wars) and given to Lt. Hutton by Mr. John Dunn. The pillow is now in the Regimental Museum.

became standard throughout the Regiment. In 1824 the motto 'Celer et Audax' was formally resumed by permission of George IV.

On the parade square, words of command were reduced to the absolute minimum, and what Liddell Hart has called 'picked line infantry, combining the steadiness of the regular with the freedom and craft of the irregular' evolved into the concept of the Rifleman. It is a concept which has survived all the technical advances which gave the rest of the infantry the weapons which the 60th pioneered.

In 1827 the Duke of York died and his brother, the

Duke of Cambridge, became Colonel-in-Chief of the Regiment. Four years later, the title 'The 60th, The King's Royal Rifle Corps' was promulgated. Six years after that, the young Victoria came to the throne, but the title of the Regiment was not altered, and it was under this designation that its various battalions took part in the Sikh War, the Kaffir War, the China War, the First Afghan War, the Zulu War and the many 'expeditions' that tested its fortitude and enterprise like Egypt, Manipur, Burma and Chitral.

As the years went by, the West Indies saw less and less of the 60th, although one battalion (the 4th, raised again in 1857) saw service in the same hemisphere, in Canada, guarding the border throughout the American Civil War. The Regiment's new battle honours reflected the changing direction of the new Empire, and it was in India that the Regiment went through what its historian has called its 'golden age'.

The 1st Battalion arrived in India too late to participate in the First Sikh War, but two years later, in 1849, when the Second erupted, it was given a chance to demonstrate its marching ability, as it moved nearly 500 miles in five weeks, fighting two major actions on the way at Mooltan and Goojerat. After that, the entire Punjab territory was annexed by Britain, and the regiment gained two new battle honours.

Thus, as 1850 signalled the half-way point in the 19th century, the 1st Battalion contributed to the mobile columns that were continually in the field, putting down tribal revolts and manning the frontier posts. In 1850, too, the Duke of Cambridge died and the Prince Consort assumed the title of Colonel-in-Chief of the Regiment, while an ageing Duke of Wellington commented on the 1st's annual inspection by writing that 'the state of this Battalion seems in the highest degree satisfactory'.

Thus reassured, the Battalion faced the future with

Officers of the 60th (circa 1845).

equanimity, little dreaming that, in 1857, all their training and resolution would be put to a cruel test.

The origins of the Great Bengal Mutiny have been closely examined by many. John Masters, in the preface to his novel, *Nightrunners of Bengal*, has summed them up succinctly:

> The mutiny was not spontaneous; it was planned, though even
> yet no one knows exactly how or by whom. It is known that
> many worked in secret—sullen princes, deprived of their despotic
> power . . . patriots, angry under the yoke; money brokers seek-
> ing profit in chaos; jealously hopeful rulers of other countries.

All these influences, and many more, worked on the key
to British rule in India: the sepoys. Superstitious and easily
alarmed by rumour, they were told that their masters were
trying to convert them to Christianity by undermining
their native religions. The spark that ignited the tinder
was the introduction of the now famous greased cartridge,
which was alleged to be coated with a combination of pig
and cow fat. The end of the cartridge had to be bitten
open to release the powder, and the animal fat thus used
to preserve it from damp was intolerable to both Hindu
and Muslim.

The 1st Battalion, stationed at Meerut, a garrison town
some forty miles north-east of Delhi, had more warning
of the revolt than most of the British units; on Sunday
evening, May 10, the Battalion was on the square, waiting
for evening church parade, the time for which had been
put back, at the last minute, by half an hour. Suddenly a
rifleman, panting with excitement, ran on to the square
with the news that the sepoys of the Indian regiments were
running amok, murdering their officers and every European they could find.

The regimental officers on parade reacted with com-
mendable speed to this appalling news. There was time to
secure the Treasury building and the Regimental Maga-
zine, issue ammunition for the new Enfield rifles which had
just been taken into use, and march towards the Native
Lines, led by the Lieutenant-Colonel on duty, John Jones.
Lewis Butler has described what they found:

> . . . a sight as thrilling as it was terrible—a city for the length
> of over a mile in flames . . . By this time the sun had set; but the

moon rose upon the lurid scene and the darkness was illuminated by the burning roofs of thatched bungalows, amid which the forms of mounted Sowars (native cavalrymen) riding furiously about with brandished swords could clearly be discerned.

The 60th officer in charge of the troops turned to his superior and asked if they were to 'shoot straight'. The answer was 'shoot them like dogs'. The volley that followed was the first fired by the British in the Mutiny.

The 60th slept with their weapons beside them that night and in the morning made a cautious reconnaissance. The mutineers had fled, dismayed that the battalion they had thought to trap unarmed in church was very much alive and active. They left behind them scenes that stunned the senses. No one had dreamt of the depths of hatred and suppressed resentment that had lain concealed beneath the seemingly loyal and willing features of the sepoys. Mutilated bodies of women and children were found everywhere, arousing the troops to a frenzy of revenge that duplicated the feelings of the rebellious native soldiery.

> . . . they came upon the corpse of Mrs. Chambers, who had recently arrived from England, and was a general favourite in society, lying in a ditch and literally cut to pieces. Horror-stricken at the sight, officers and men raised their weapons in the air and vowed to avenge her death.

Before long, the 1st Battalion was known to the mutineers as the Regiment from Hell. Their Lieutenant-Colonel, John Jones, became known throughout the whole army, on both sides, as 'Jones the Avenger'.

Hate begets hate, and outrage outrage. The savagery that followed, as Delhi was overwhelmed and captured by the mutineers, was practised by both sides. No quarter was the order of the day. The vengeance of Victorian England, which had prided itself on the tolerance of its benign rule, and had been lulled into complacency by its apparent success, was the more terrible because its rule had been rejected. Britain had brought peace, justice, modern transportation and western civilization to a sub-continent that seemed to need it desperately, only to find that the people did not want it. This was the bitter blow.

In fairness, it must be remembered that not all of India succumbed to the intoxication of violent action; the Sikhs, whose territory had been so recently 'integrated' into British India, remained loyal and the Gurkhas were another source of strength. But the inexorable fact remained that some 22,000 British troops were awash in a sub-continent screaming for their blood, and facing 150,000 natives who had been trained with loving care in the use of all the modern weapons of war.

The siege and recapture of Delhi has always been regarded by The King's Royal Rifle Corps as an epic event

The 60th at the storming of Delhi.

in its long history. The mistakes made by the administrators, that undoubtedly precipitated the Mutiny, were not made by the British garrisons. Their relations with the native troops were, on the whole, warm and friendly. After the Mutiny it was different; there were too many horrors to forget. But in 1857 the event was unbelievable because there seemed to be no reason for it, and the 60th was in the indignant van that sought to retrieve the British position in India, while punishing severely those who had sought to destroy it.

The recapture of Delhi was the most urgent need. To some at home in England, the desperate romance of besieged Lucknow, and its ultimate relief, was the great saga of the whole sorry affair, but Delhi, capital city of the old Mogul Empire, was a symbol to the native insurgents; as long as it remained in their hands the Mutiny had not been defeated and all India might be encouraged to rise in arms.

It was a very curious siege. The British and their loyal levies were too small a force to invest a city seven miles in circumference. They could only sit on a ridge to the north of it and invite attack from enraged sepoys who dared not sit idle; every day brought reinforcement nearer.

The original column that was ordered south from Meerut to attack Delhi was almost laughably small. The 1st Battalion of the 60th was the main force, supported by two squadrons of cavalry and a few guns. The total strength seems to have been less than 1,000. Against them were 20,000 well-armed sepoys who were daily being augmented as more mutineers marched to the defence of the Imperial City. In spite of the disparity of size, the column from Meerut drove back all attempts to keep it away and steadily grew nearer.

As it fought its way south, individual units marched in to help. The 2nd Gurkhas, who were warmly welcomed and whose relations with the 60th during the siege became so close that they afterwards asked for, and were granted, permission to wear the same uniform, were among the first to appear; it is significant that this tradition of friendliness still stands, and the 2nd Gurkhas not only continue to wear green but also possess one part of the table which was used at the time for casualties, the other two parts belonging respectively to The King's Royal Rifle Corps and to the Guides. The 'Delhi Field Force', after further reinforcements, finally grew large enough for

Various headgear worn by the 60th over the years displayed on the section of the table used during the siege of Delhi for the treatment of casualties.

someone to be sent to command it, and a succession of Generals made their appearance, only to fall sick of cholera and be replaced. By mid-June the Force was 4,000 strong and had established itself on the Ridge, well dug in.

Two landmarks defined the position: Flag Staff Tower to the east and Hindoo Rau's house to the west. From the moment of their occupation of this position, the British were under continual attack, as forays by thousands of sepoys were made, week after week, from the safe haven that was Delhi. All were beaten back. With July, the rains came and with them a marked increase of malaria and

61

Hindoo Rau's house, a post of the 60th during the Siege of Delhi in 1857.

cholera. The 1st Battalion escaped much of the effect of these diseases; they were old India hands, and seemed immune. Their problem was the daily wastage from the constant fighting, and a draft of 200, arriving from Calcutta, was a welcome addition.

The Commanding Officer, Lieutenant-Colonel John Jones, was prominent throughout the defence of the Ridge. He never lost the determination to subdue the mutineers and avenge the murder of so many helpless innocents. His men were infected with his resolve. 'Our men,' wrote one officer, 'are thought a great deal of, and certainly they are beautiful shots; the enemy funks us more than any other regiment, so much so that the King of Delhi has offered a reward for every Rifleman's jacket brought into Delhi.'

As July ended and the heat of August followed, the civilian authorities began to press the commander of the Delhi Field Force for a victory. No one knew better than Brigadier-General Archdale Wilson that there was an urgent need to capture Delhi. A senior gunner, he had barely escaped the fury of the mutineers at Meerut and had assumed command after officers more senior to him had succumbed to sickness and strain. But his force was still pathetically small and a defeat would mean a spread of the disaffection to all of northern India. He asked for more, especially a siege train. Reluctantly, more troops were sent, including heavy guns, until he had about 8,000 at his command. It was not too many; by this time the number of troops within the city varied between 40,000 and 60,000.

At the end of the first week in September the attack began and within a week the siege guns were ripping breaches in the walls. On September 14, in searing heat, the main attack went in.

Colonel Jones and his riflemen were in the van. Their role, as usual, was skirmishing, their task, keeping the enemy on the walls from engaging the columns of advancing infantry. The Colonel had 'inspected his Battalion as minutely as if it had been on the parade square at Meerut'. General Wilson, who was observing from the

A group of 60th officers photographed inside the Palace of Delhi just after the capture. 'Jones the Avenger', with the white beard, is seated in the centre.

battery which had caused the main breach, had told the column commander to 'advance when you hear the rifles open fire'. It was now well past dawn. Wilson leaned over the bastion protecting the guns and said, quietly, 'Now, Colonel Jones'.

A great cheer broke the silence as the riflemen surged forward. In no time they reached the foot of the wall and began picking off the defenders above them. The columns followed swiftly and, although thinned by grape shot and musket fire, fought through the breaches and into the town. There, the lack of numbers told and they were soon involved in confused house-to-house fighting in the narrow streets. The struggle that followed ebbed and flowed; the sepoys fought stubbornly and well. But the attackers had been given clear objectives and slowly fought towards them. The 60th, forgetting that their task had ended with the successful storming of the walls, joined in.

'Jones the Avenger' had his eye on the Royal Palace and worked steadily towards it, clearing house after house on the way. On the 20th, six days after the attack began, sappers got to the Palace gate under the protecting fire of the 60th, blew it open, and the riflemen, led by Jones, surged in. Once inside, he called for silence and drank a toast to the Queen's health.

At dawn the next day, as the sepoy garrison streamed away from the city in full flight, the Imperial City was once again in British hands.

The 60th lost 92 all ranks killed and wounded in the siege of Delhi. This total, when added to the numbers lost during the whole of the Mutiny, amounted to sixty per cent of their strength. If one leaves out the draft that reached them during the siege, three-quarters of the officers and men who marched out of Meerut in May became casualties. Seven Victoria Crosses were earned by members of the 1st Battalion during the campaign.

With Delhi regained and the last Mogul Emperor in

exile, the Mutiny faltered. Roving columns of British and loyal natives gradually restored order to the devastated territory. It was not until September that the 1st Battalion, armed with a new weapon, the short Enfield rifle, got a real rest. In March 1860 it embarked for England, having served in India for fifteen years.

The 2nd Battalion, stationed at the time of the Mutiny in Cape Colony, was sent to India in 1858 and served in several pacifying columns. Thereafter, it was sent to China, there to serve for over a year in that ill-conceived expedition sent to force more trade on the Chinese. Fighting a vastly superior force, in a hostile country many thousands of miles from home, it carried out all its assignments gallantly and well. As a reward, each man received £4 in prize money from the loot of the Summer Palace of the Chinese Emperor. By the spring of 1862, the 2nd Battalion was back in England.

Thereafter, fourteen years elapsed before a rifleman of the 60th fired a shot in anger except during the Fenian Raids of 1866; garrison duty absorbed them, in Malta, Madras, Egypt and Canada. During this period the personality and ability of Lieutenant-Colonel Robert Beaufoy Hawley dominated the world of the The King's Royal Rifle Corps. Though he was never tested in battle, his reforms, methods of training and high standards became legendary. As C.O. of the 4th Battalion, stationed in Canada, he encouraged all ranks to live and work as individuals in the forests and wilds that still surrounded the garrison towns. His ideas were in the same tradition as those of Bouquet and de Rothenburg, and his place among the regimental great is assured for all time. He died in 1898, as the South African War loomed on the British horizon. During the last decades of his life, various battalions of the 60th had seen service in the Second Afghan War, particularly during Roberts' celebrated march from Kabul to Kandahar, in the abortive war against the Boers in 1881,

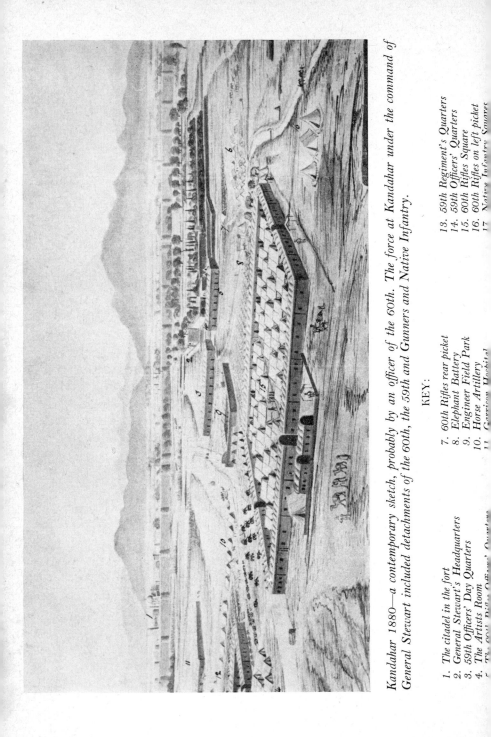

Kandahar 1880—a contemporary sketch, probably by an officer of the 60th. The force at Kandahar under the command of General Stewart included detachments of the 60th, the 59th and Gunners and Native Infantry.

KEY:

1. The citadel in the fort
2. General Stewart's Headquarters
3. 59th Officers' Day Quarters
4. The Artists Room
5. The 60th Rifles Officers' Quarters
7. 60th Rifles rear picket
8. Elephant Battery
9. Engineer Field Park
10. Horse Artillery
11. Garrison Hospital
13. 59th Regiment's Quarters
14. 59th Officers' Quarters
15. 60th Rifles Square
16. 60th Rifles on left picket
17. Native Infantry Squares

Lieutenant-Colonel Robert Beaufoy Hawley.

at Tel-el-Kebir and on the North-West Frontier of India, in Burma and in Chitral; three Victoria Crosses were won during these campaigns, all of which tested the Regiment severely but successfully. The experience gained by the 60th proved to be only too valuable when the South African War broke out.

The 1st Battalion on parade at Peshawar in March 1895.

Chapter 5

It's time to do and dare, Dolly Gray.

MUSIC HALL SONG

SOMEONE ONCE SAID that there is nothing like a war to upset an army. He must have been speaking of the South African War. There, an army that had followed British mercantile expansion around the world for generations, with almost unqualified success, came face to face with a real war, with white antagonists, armed with modern weapons, and almost foundered.

The 60th participated in this unwelcome and costly campaign in a curious way; due to its multiplicity of battalions it came in bit by bit. Its battle honour, Ladysmith, is unique, for two battalions underwent the tortures of the siege, while two more (one a temporary unit made up of reinforcements) were in the relieving force.

While Lord Roberts, Kitchener and French made their dramatic moves in Central South Africa, The King's Royal Rifle Corps suffered through the so-called 'Eastern' campaign, directed at the relief of Ladysmith. It is ironic that much of their suffering came as a result of the well-meaning blunderings of one of their own: General Sir Redvers Buller. He had had a spectacular career in his youth, winning the Victoria Cross, and had undoubtedly been a fine leader greatly admired by his troops, but the new tactics employed in South Africa exposed his weakness and his fifteen years spent in staff work gave him little assistance in his role as a field commander.

When Buller sailed from England at the head of a Corps

The Wreck of The Warren Hastings (Not referred to in the text)

On the night of the 14th January 1897, in pitch darkness and pouring rain, the troopship Warren Hastings on her way from Cape Town to Mauritius, steaming at full speed, struck the rocks off the Island of Reunion. On board were the H.Q. and four companies of the 1st Battalion which, together with other Military detachments, women and children totalled 995. They* at once fell in on the main deck in perfect order until 4 a.m. when the (Naval) Commander ordered disembarkation to commence by rope ladders from the bows. . . . At 4.20 a.m. the position of the vessel appeared so critical that he at once ordered the disembarkation of the men to cease, and the women, children and sick to be passed out. This order was promptly carried out; the men clung to the side as they stood, the ship lurching and bumping heavily, and passed out the women and children through the foreport; no man murmuring or moving from his post."

A few minutes later, as the ship was in imminent danger of heeling over and sinking, it became necessary to expedite the landing. Owing to the 'remarkable courage and exemplary discipline' displayed, the whole ship's company, except two natives, were safely passed on to the rocks and saved.

Vide Regimental Chronicle, 1909.

of four divisions, ample cavalry and sufficient artillery, it seemed only a matter of time before the affair would be terminated. But, concealed beneath the pageantry of the departure, seeds of trouble were germinating. None of the commanders had been practised in high command, there was no proper general staff, communications were inadequate, and few had thought out the tactics of fighting a highly mobile enemy in trackless, open country.

Further, no one had dared, for a generation, to oppose seriously the advance of a British force as imposing as Buller's. When the Boers did oppose it, incredibly, a plan had to be made, and plans involving so many troops were complicated things that demanded a staff which in this case was lacking. Instead of a solemn march through terrified communities, Buller found himself face to face with an adversary as well armed as he was, and far more determined.

The South African War, or rather the British memory of it, seems shadowy now, although it only happened sixty-eight years ago. If one may hazard a guess, the average knowledge of it is confined to the facts that Lord Roberts won it, that the Boers fought bravely, that Ladysmith was besieged and relieved, that the Boers were treated magnanimously afterwards and the British permitted the election of General Smuts as Prime Minister, even though he had been a Boer leader.

This is accurate enough as far as it goes, but it is hardly enough. What is not generally recalled, for example, is that at the height of the war Britain and the Empire had 250,000 men deployed against a Boer force that never numbered more than 60,000, yet found it difficult to force a decision.

It was the first 'modern' war fought by Britain. The armies were equipped with rifled cannon, shrapnel shells, machine-guns, barbed wire and mines. The troops wore khaki, carried Lee Metford or Lee Enfield rifles and the telegraph and telephone were available for communication.

It is a pity that the most suitable general to command this force was deemed to be sixty-year-old Redvers Buller, kindly, heavily built and fumbling. He took on personal direction of the Relief of Ladysmith, was defeated in the field, and as a result forfeited his position as Commander-in-Chief. Lord Roberts was sent out, with more troops, to fill this role, leaving Buller to deal with his Ladysmith problem.

Things improved when Lord Roberts arrived, but until he did, the Expeditionary Force, and the 60th, suffered deeply.

Hostilities opened in October 1899 with an advance into the east coast colony of Natal by a force of some 14,000 Boer horsemen from the Transvaal. Opposing them, 12,000 British regulars, including the 1st and 2nd K.R.R.C., were dispersed in mixed forces guarding frontier towns.

The first clash occured as the Boers, under Joubert,

General Sir Redvers Buller, V.C., 'Kindly, heavily built and fumbling'.

headed for the northern coal-mining village of Dundee, defended by 4,000 men under Major-General Sir W. Penn Symons, who soon found himself threatened on three sides. In spite of this, a strange atmosphere of 'business as usual' was maintained.

Rayne Kruger, writing of the 'invasion', says that Joubert could not believe it, and looked for a cunning trap:

> No passes were mined, tunnels blocked or bridges blown up. The railway line (to Pretoria, capital of the Transvaal) was left untouched.

The British had made no use of the priceless defence that the mountains along the border offered them.

By the evening of October 19, the Boers had closed in on Dundee but Penn Symons, though warned by outlying picquets, refused to believe that it was more than a raid. Kruger has described Symons' disillusionment:

> When the camp awoke at daybreak the surrounding hill tops were obscured in a swirling mist. After 5 a.m. morning parade the artillery horses were led away to water a mile away, and the men busied themselves with the usual camp fatigues before breakfast. Suddenly the mist lifted, the whole crestline of Talana and the adjoining hill was seen crammed with Boers, outlined against the pale eastern light.

What happened next is almost unbelievable. Penn Symons decided to attack Talana Hill. Kruger comments: 'Fortune is apt to favour the foolish as well as the brave. Symons being both, he was abundantly favoured.' Surrounded on three sides, outnumbered and outgunned, he sent his men off against the first Boers he could see.

The 1st K.R.R.C. participated in the ensuing attack, first in a supporting role, its accurate rifle fire on the crest enabling the leading troops to get to the foot of the hill. Then it was their turn and the very speed with which they raced upward saved casualties. The Boer line began to waver and fall back, more infantry moved up to support the 60th and, in spite of an artillery mistake that lobbed shells into the advancing British infantry, the hill was taken by sword and bayonet. The Commanding Officer of the 60th, Lieutenant-Colonel R. Gunning, was killed in the final assault. Penn Symons suffered a mortal wound in the early stages of his strange attack.

The Battle of Talana Hill, taken in isolation, was a brilliant success. A formidable Boer force was driven from a commanding position by troops that had been taken by surprise. But had the other Boer troops been in position, too, this rash assault would have resulted in disaster.

As it was, the known presence of the rest of the Boer invaders, determined by some inconclusive cavalry encounters, persuaded Penn Symons' successor, Yule, and the commander at Ladysmith, Sir George White, that the time had come to concentrate the outlying troops. A general retirement to Ladysmith was ordered.

The resulting trek south, in teeming rain, was a nightmare to troops exhausted by battle, but after three days and nights of marching the Dundee detachment joined the main force where the 2nd Battalion, newly arrived, was waiting to greet the weary 1st. The 60th historian, in commenting on the Dundee affair, sets the scene for the sorry performances to follow:

> Sent out, no one knows why, to do no one knows what, they had inflicted a smart defeat on one portion of greatly superior forces seeking to overwhelm them, shown that they could turn a Boer force of equal numbers out of a strong position, and had then . . . slipped clean away . . . without losing a man or a wagon.

In brief, the troops were fine—it was the generalship that was lacking. This was amply demonstrated when, on October 30, Sir George White attempted to brush aside the Boer encirclement of Ladysmith. The plan was too complicated, the orders too casual and the enemy too

A Naval 12-pounder gun, ingeniously adapted for use in the field.

efficient. The attack was thrown back on the town and the siege began in earnest. The British lost 1,200 badly needed men; the Boers, about 200. Both sides had long-range guns; a detachment of Royal Naval gunners with several ingeniously adapted 12-pounder guns arrived at the last moment before the encirclement was complete but the Boers' 'Long Tom', dragged south by oxen, balanced and outranged everything but these. The defenders of Lady-smith settled down to it secure in the knowledge that help was arriving at Durban, less than 150 miles away.

When Buller arrived in the Cape Colony with his newly organized Corps, he found British garrisons beleaguered in three towns, Ladysmith, Kimberley and Mafeking, and the security of the Cape threatened by marauding Boer commandos. His force was not large enough to relieve all three places simultaneously, so he left small forces in the Cape Colony to maintain what pressure they could on the Boers of the Orange Free State, and sailed off to Durban with the remainder. Natal, he felt, was the most seriously threatened point.

As soon as the troops arrived, they were sent forward in the direction of Ladysmith. The Boers had not attempted to advance in strength beyond the Ingela River, about fourteen miles south of the besieged city, although their patrols had penetrated to within a few miles of Durban, capturing in the process young Mr. Winston Churchill.

Slowly and methodically Buller, handicapped by having only his personal staff with him, built up his strength along the Tugela, preparatory to a drive north to Ladysmith.

It took him three months and four massive tries to do it. In the process, he lost more men that the total number of Boers opposing him, yet part of his hesitation was a dread of high casualties.

In Kruger's words 'Buller had but to do things right once, only once' to be instantly successful. Instead, a

A Cartoon from the Ladysmith Lyre, a journal circulated in the besieged town to raise morale.

succession of half-hearted attacks wearied his troops and exasperated his subordinates.

The 60th suffered through all these ineptly handled battles. At Colenso, they were ordered to withdraw when it seemed perfectly feasible to remain where they were, and at Spion Kop their successful attack on the Twin Peaks was a model of its kind and held the key to victory. It was at Colenso, incidentally, that Lieutenant The Hon. Frederick Hugh Sherston Roberts of the K.R.R.C., son of Lord Roberts, won his V.C. in a gallant attempt to save the guns from under the very muzzles of the Boer rifles. This was the first recorded case of the son of a V.C. (Lord Roberts had won his in India in 1858) being similarly decorated.

The Twin Peaks battle was a part of the fight for Spion Kop. When that attack bogged down, the 3rd Battalion, K.R.R.C., was ordered by its Divisional Commander to widen the front and prevent the Boers on the Peaks from reinforcing those counter-attacking Spion Kop.

A Boer commando group of 200 men was dug in and camouflaged on the Twin Peaks. The 3rd Battalion forded the Tugela during the morning and at 2 p.m. began to advance over the open ground between the river and the foot of the hills, moving in open order, 'each company deployed in two lines, a half company in each, at eight or ten paces interval, with 150 yards between lines'. In this extended order they advanced over a mile and a half, coming under Boer fire about half way and breaking into the double. At the foot of the hill the fire grew hotter, but under the protection of a deep gulley the men were organized into groups of twenty and rushed forward to the dead ground at the very foot of the hill, where they began the climb to the top.

The slope was steep and exposed in several places to cross-fire; casualties occurred at these spots. But the advance was maintained. 'Crawling, climbing, running, firing from every rock and at every opportunity, the Riflemen worked their way up the hill. When our men got to within 150 yards of the summit the Boers gave up the struggle and fled.' By 5.30 both peaks were firmly held. The Commanding Officer, Colonel Buchanan Riddell, was shot dead by a Boer marksman on the very crest of the ridge.

Alas, the battlefield initiative taken by their divisional commander that had prompted the advance annoyed Buller and he ordered them withdrawn. As the Boers streamed northwards in defeat, the 3rd Battalion marched down their hill and recrossed the Tugela. Victory had been lost through pique, and when the Boers learned of the withdrawal, they turned about and reoccupied their former lines. The 60th lost three officers and nineteen other ranks killed, four officers and seventy-three other ranks wounded. The next day (January 26) all the British had fallen back to the security of the south bank of the Tugela.

On February 5 Buller tried once more. Again he threw a part of his force against a piece of the enemy's line, a hill called Vaal Krant. Again the troops (four battalions of light infantry and rifles, one of which was the 3rd K.R.R.C.) captured their objective, again Buller lost his nerve and ordered them back across the Tugela.

For the fourth try, the Rifle Reserve Battalion, made up of reinforcements intended for the two 60th Battalions and the 2nd Rifle Brigade in Ladysmith, came forward and joined the 11th Brigade. This time Buller used his whole force against the Boer line, though by no means simultaneously. What should have been done in a day and a half took nearly five and the Boers were driven back, not routed. By the evening of February 28, the Boer line along the Tugela had been breached at every point and the way lay open to Ladysmith. It took until March 3 to march the fourteen miles that remained. Buller was not the man to hurry, especially when there seemed no need to do so.

Prices ran high in besieged Ladysmith.

During the 114 days of the siege, the Boers made only one attempt to carry Ladysmith by storm. On January 6, 1900 they sent 4,000 men against a key point in the defence, Caesar's Camp and Wagon Hill. The battle was touch and go throughout the day and the last garrison reserves were thrown in at the end, including, of course, both 60th Battalions. But as darkness fell and a thunderstorm added to the confusion, the Boers abandoned the attack and streamed back to their lines of encircling trenches. Thereafter, they relied on the cumulative effect of short rations, falling stocks of ammunition and disease to effect the reduction of Ladysmith. Buller's belated arrival frustrated this aim.

The rest of the campaign in Natal savoured of anticlimax as Lord Roberts stole the headlines with his advance through the Orange Free State. Buller's force was depleted by Roberts' call for troops, leaving him with about 15,000 men. He moved northwards during April and May, closing up to the mountain barrier and shepherding Boer rearguards ahead of him. First one pass and then the next was cleared as the Boers gave up the attempt to figh pitched battles with the British and the period of the commando raids began.

The lines of communication had now to be garrisoned, while mixed columns were formed to find and bring Boer columns to battle. This was more easily planned than accomplished for the slow-moving British columns, chained to their unwieldy supply trains, could only hope to push back the mobile Boer rearguards; it was impossible to bring them to battle.

On October 2, Buller received word of his recall to England. The regimental historian has written:

> Never, through the worst of his failures, had he lost for one moment the confidence and affection of his troops. Never did the most successful of Generals receive a more touching and heartfelt ovation than did he on his departure for home.

In July 1900, the 2nd Battalion had left South Africa as an escort for Boer prisoners-of-war destined for Ceylon. The rest of the 60th participated in 'mobile column' activity, and the gruelling work of building 'the block-house lines' designed to fragment and trap the remnants of the Boer commandos. In one of these actions a V.C. was won by Lieutenant L. A. E. Price-Davies of the K.R.R.C. Like Lieutenant Roberts, Price-Davies was also attempting to save the guns from capture but unlike Roberts he lived to tell the tale.

At the time Lieutenant Price-Davies was serving with the Mounted Infantry which had been created and fostered by Captain (later Lieutenant-General Sir Edward) Hutton of the 60th.

This new arm was taken up with enthusiasm by the descendants of Bouquet's riflemen as it was in the direct tradition of all his teaching i.e. to act as scouts and the eyes of the army by quick thinking, quick moving and good concealment and shooting.

Companies of MI were formed by some other Regiments but more officers and men were provided by the 60th than by any other Regiment and in 1901 a complete Battalion (25th MI Bn) was formed from MI Companies of the 1st, 3rd and 4th Battalions.

In Pretoria, late at night on May 31, 1902, nearly three years after the war began, the Boers acknowledged defeat and signed a treaty of peace. Queen Victoria had been queen when it began. Edward VII was on the throne when it ended. Everyone was glad that the Boer War was over. Few wondered why it had been necessary in the first place.

The war had a significant effect on the British Army. Unlike its European neighbours, who had been squabbling

A Guard of Honour at the Rifle Depot for the funeral of Queen Victoria. The 60th are in front and behind them a detachment from the Rifle Brigade.

with modern weapons for years, Britain had been maintaining the security of her overseas possessions with a minimum of technical aids and a maximum of military gallantry. The war in South Africa demonstrated that this was not enough, and, with the Empire quiet again, the only enemies in sight were European. The army began to modernize and the traditions of the 60th were available as tested techniques. The accumulated regimental experience, won over 150 years of colonial adventure, became for the first time formalized in South Africa. Riflemen were expected by now to march faster and longer, shoot straighter, use cover, advance at speed to the objective, and do it all with a minimum of casualties. 'Celer et Audax' was now a way of life for all ranks of the 60th.

Chapter 6

The new troops follow after, and tread the land we won,
To them 'tis so much hillside, re-wrested from the Hun;
We only walk with reverence this sullen mile of mud;
The shell-holes hold our history, and half of them our blood.

A. P. HERBERT

THE ORIGINS OF the First World War (called the Great War until the Second erupted) have been studied by scholars for over fifty years; the Allied view held at the time, of a hungry, power-mad Germany seeking to conquer the world, has long since been modified. Reflection, and the availability of official records, have at least done that. But from the point of view of a British regiment who went through it the origins hardly matter. It happened, it was most unpleasant, and, somehow, the British were on the winning side.

The Regular Army was as ready for a European war as recent experience could ensure. The South African adventure had shaken the complacent at the Horse Guards and a new air of professional competence had blown away much of the dust. The only ingredient lacking was foresight; no one thought much of machine-guns, and as for artillery, it was felt to be of real value only when used against half-trained troops. The shock power of the bayonet had made the Boers run, and what were Boers but agile Germans? The years of 'attrition' facing the contending armies were not expected by either side. Indeed, under the circumstances, it is hard to see how anyone could have expected them. The German victories of the late 19th century had been swift and sure, and it was widely believed that no modern state could fight a long war; they were too interdependent.

It is difficult to write of the First World War with any degree of detachment; a generation died in its battles. Generalship at the higher level on both sides was bad and, far too often, men were thrown into action to retrieve reputations, with all the desperation of a heavy loser at the gaming tables of Monte Carlo.

The badges of The King's Royal Rifle Corps were worn by more men than in any previous war; there were seventeen active battalions, brought up to strength after each battle by reinforcements provided largely by the nine reserve battalions in England. When one remembers that it was quite usual to lose one-third to one-half of a battalion in an attack, one's senses stagger when confronted by the cost.

For a while, the pre-war training counted; the British Expeditionary Force that landed in France in August 1914 was armed with the short Lee-Enfield, a useful bolt-action rifle that could be used to get off fifteen shots per minute in the hands of trained soldiers. In the first actions around Mons and Le Cateau, the German assault troops thought that they were up against massive machine-gun fire. Alas, the 'grey-green hordes' had real machine-guns which soon dominated the battlefield, and when the Schlieffen strategy failed, and the war took on the aspects of siege on an enormous scale, the German superiority in weaponry dominated subsequent operations for the next two years.

As trench warfare deepened, demands for victory grew loud, but the means of achieving it—a decisive superiority at some point along the line—continued to elude both sides. In trying for it, the British, lacking the sophisticated weaponry of later years, used their only asset, manpower. Armies became battering-rams made up of human flesh, and all the skills acquired so painstakingly by regiments like the 60th were put aside. With England near, and a whole population to draw on, casualties became, for the first time, a secondary preoccupation.

84

The Regiment suffered throughout most of the war from this misuse of trained manpower. It was only in the opening stages, in the first three glorious weeks of manoeuvre, that it had a chance to pit its skill in open country against the German enemy.

The 1st Battalion was the first unit of the Regiment to test the opponent's skill. The 1st had marched away from Mons with the rest of the B.E.F., but had not seen much fighting. On September 10, however, as the British turned and began to advance, the leading brigade of the 2nd Division bumped into a German battalion acting as a rearguard near the village of Hautesvesnes, north of the Marne. The troops in the lead were ordered to hold the village against flank attack and the 1st K.R.R.C. was ordered to attack the German rearguard. A battery of 18-pounders clattered up to give support and the assault went in. It was done in perfect textbook style. The Riflemen advanced swiftly by fire and movement, outclassing and overwhelming the Germans, hundreds of whom surrendered.

Later in the week, on September 14, the 2nd Battalion had a similar encounter, when, as part of the 1st Division, its accuracy and skilful use of cover drove off Germans defending a ridge covering the Chemin des Dames. But the Germans had retired as far as they intended and the subsequent struggle to retain the ground presaged the onset of trench warfare. Once the German guns and machine-guns came forward it was necessary to dig in to survive and another stretch was added to the long line of defences growing from Switzerland north-westward to the sea. The techniques of manœuvre, so painstakingly taught, were soon forgotten in this new war, waged by whole nations in arms on a battlefield stretching for hundreds of miles with no flanks to turn, and no empty roads on which to move armies.

The years that followed, as the generals sought to

overcome this totally unexpected development, became endless eons of frustration. Few old hands survived the early battles to recall the days of excellence; for the 60th, soon expanded by the addition of many new battalions, the war became little more than a test of courage. There was so little opportunity for skill. In 1915, the 4th Battalion lost half its strength at St. Eloi, the 1st was shattered at Givenchy, and in June the 7th, 8th and 9th Battalions were decimated withstanding a savage German attack and then lost further hundreds in a badly co-ordinated counter-attack. As the thickets of barbed wire grew (no way of cutting it effectively was found until 1917), so did the heaps of dead in front as men strove, under fire, to creep under it, or climb over it or tear it aside with their bare hands. This was the bleak pattern of events as 1915 came and went. It is impossible to pick out a special figure from this period and say 'this was a regimental hero'. They were all heroes. Commanding officers were killed or wounded before they could really know their men, and the average life of a junior officer was measured in weeks, not months. As for the men, they often died before they had even seen a senior officer.

When one studies these battles, like Loos in September, it is impossible to avoid a feeling of black rage at the folly of them. Brave men gave their lives freely to correct slack staff work and slovenly preparation. Neither the higher commanders nor their staffs had ever handled such masses of men and they did it badly from the first. The British nation had slid into war inadequately prepared for the larger consequences and she had the generals she deserved: the ones who were prepared to serve in the armies of those days. The officers and men of the regiments did their best to carry out the orders they received. Their incredible gallantry retrieved the Somme, in 1916, from utter failure.

In the Regiment's *Brief History* (a paper-back synop-

sis), a laconic statement prefaces a description of 1916:
'The Somme battle opened on 1st July. Fourteen battalions
of the Regiment were ultimately engaged in it.'

The Battle of the Somme lasted for months. Time after
time the various battalions of the 60th managed somehow
to get through the wire and reach the enemy lines. Time
after time they had to withdraw 'because of failure on the
flanks'. The reason for the failure was simple enough: the
units on the flanks had ceased to exist, eliminated by
enemy machine-gun fire. By November it was over and,
as the survivors trudged away to try elsewhere, they could
take some consolation from the fact that they had done

*Sergeant W. Mortimer M.M. and L/Cpl. L. Harris of the 60th—
members of the 1st Division in France 1916–1917.*

Coalbox, mascot of the 2nd Bn. of the 60th on the Albert–Amiens road in September 1916.

their best. The 60th had won ten battle honours and lost 200 officers and 4,000 men.

It had been a battle of rifles and raw courage against machine-guns and artillery. The bankrupt policy of attrition, resorted to by generals who would not wait for shells and could not admit their inability to solve the problem in any other way, resulted in British casualties of more than 400,000. The enemy, too, had suffered grievously, but in the words of one historian, 'we cannot close our eyes to the horror of the mass butchery to which the C.-in-C's [Sir Douglas Haig's] tactics had condemned the troops under his command'.

The opening battles of the year 1917 were better. At long last the shells began to arrive, and the big guns. A fuse that would permit the heavy guns to cut wire had been

88

developed and, after Vimy Ridge and the opening phases of the First Battle of Arras, there was hope of more intelligent conduct of the war. Several battalions of the Regiment were involved, notably the 9th, on the opening day of the battle. The wire facing it had been cut, and with comparatively light cost the battalion swept over the German lines that were its objective and secured many prisoners and weapons. The fighting around Arras had been intended to draw German strength away from the Aisne front, in order to assist the French general Nivelle in his big offensive; but security was lost, the Germans knew the plan and Nivelle failed disastrously. Haig turned his attention to his favourite project, an advance from the Ypres salient intended to capture the small channel ports of Zeebrugge and Ostend, where German 'U' boats harboured.

Haig could extract obedience from the troops under his command, but like Canute, control of the elements was beyond him. The battle started in a downpour of rain and ended in muddy ruin.

As usual, the battle began well. The capture of Messines Ridge was an essential preliminary, for it dominated the whole salient. General Plumer, an able leader in whom the 60th had great confidence, flung his Second Army at it after careful planning, including the exploding of several enormous mines placed in tunnels under the German lines and good artillery preparation. It was a complete success.

Two battalions of the 60th, the 18th and 21st, participated as part of the 122nd Brigade in the 41st Division. The 21st attacked first, on June 7, 1917. A week later the 18th went into action with the last phase of the attack. The casualties in both battalions were light, many prisoners were captured and the new positions were successfully held against counter-attack. Messines, like Vimy, should have taught the High Command a lesson; when properly planned, on suitable ground, against enemy positions that had been studied in detail, success was obtainable. Unfortunately, like the Bourbon Kings of France, the High Command forgot nothing and learned nothing.

Between this operation and the beginning of the Third Battle of Ypres, the 2nd Battalion was almost wiped out defending gallantly a position it had taken over from the French on the coast. At Nieuport Bains, on the Yser River, its positions were attacked by an entire German Marine Division. At dawn on July 10, the enemy bombardment opened and continued throughout the day, beating down breastworks made of sand. There was no counter-battery fire, for the English heavy guns had not come up before the French guns were withdrawn, and there was no British reaction to the swarms of German planes that flew almost at ground level to strafe the 60th position. At 7.15 p.m. the German Marines attacked. The result was predictable.

During a lull in the battle transport of the 60th delivers officers' kit near Feuchy Cross Roads in April 1917.

Although the defenders took a heavy toll of their enemy, the position was overrun. The colonel was killed and all but eight of his officers were killed or wounded. Of the eight, five were taken prisoner. Only about forty all ranks managed to escape after the battle.

On July 31, 1917, ten days after a reluctant War Cabinet had given Haig permission to open the attack, the Third Battle of Ypres or, as it has come to be known, the Battle of Passchendaele began. Haig had said, in written support of his plan, that he had 'no intention of entering into a tremendous offensive involving heavy losses'. It is surely fair to wonder just what the dour Scot in charge of Britain's armies in the West would have considered a 'tremendous offensive'. After a bombardment lasting twelve days, which reduced the already soggy battlefield to muddy pulp, some twelve divisions were launched at the ridge delineated by the Belgian villages of Staden and Passchendaele.

Eight battalions of the Regiment saw action in the ensuing carnage, the 8th, 10th, 11th, 12th, 16th, 17th, 18th and 21st. Their daily struggles with the mud, so horribly reminiscent of the Somme, went on until September when they were pulled out one by one, to recuperate as best they could. The 60th earned seven battle honours at Third Ypres. They left behind them a battle still in progress, for, in the words of the Regimental Historian: 'The battle dragged on, as had that of the Somme, and met with the same fate—drowned out.'

The best estimate of British losses at Passchendaele is in the vicinity of 250,000. The Germans lost about 200,000. While it ground on (the Canadians finally captured the battered village on November 10), last-minute preparations for a very different operation were being completed. General Byng's Third Army was about to make its own very special kind of history and four battalions of the 60th were to participate. The target was Cambrai.

Byng was an original thinker; his whole career, from his days as a commander of irregular cavalry in South Africa, to his coup in evacuating the forces from the Dardanelles in the face of the Turkish defences, had shown great imagination. At Vimy Ridge he had demonstrated his ability as an enterprising corps commander; when given the task of capturing Cambrai, he demanded and got the one element that had been lacking from most of the previous British attacks: surprise. Sir Basil Liddell Hart attempted to emphasize, after the war, the importance of surprise in war, only to meet again the cool reception that new ideas received during it. He has said: 'A commander who selects the offensive and fails to surprise his opponent has lost the main advantage which the offensive confers.' Byng would have agreed with that. He demanded, and got, 300 tanks to lead the assault, and with this firepower and the tanks' ability to clear paths through wire, he refused any preliminary bombardment.

Some experts have declared that Cambrai was conceived as a massive raid designed to test the efficiency of tanks used in quantity; if so, it succeeded beyond its planners' wildest dreams. Had there been fresh reserves to man the trenches gained by the attackers, there is little doubt that a major breakthrough would have been feasible. But, as usual, the competence of individual army commanders did not extend higher, and the success was permitted to deteriorate into failure through lack of a quick follow-up.

The Battle of Cambrai, 1917, began on November 20, and within twenty-four hours the attackers had captured about the same amount of German-held territory as had the four-month offensive at Passchendaele. Heavy fog added to the surprise when, at 6.20 a.m., 342 tanks crossed no-man's-land followed by waves of infantry close behind along the paths cut in the wire by the five-mile-per-hour juggernauts. The 12th Battalion's war diarist found time to record a vivid picture of the beginning of it:

> The long line of tanks, magnified to monstrous size by the dim
> light of early dawn, the columns of infantry with fixed bayonets
> which followed them, all advancing silently and in order, formed
> a spectacle which no one who saw it can ever forget.

German reaction, which came slowly as they realized
what was about to happen to them, was weakened by a
smoke screen laid down by the guns, followed by heavy
artillery fire along the front of the assault. In no time the
12th Battalion was well into the Hindenburg Line, capturing trenches, prisoners and weapons. 'A' Company
got a German canteen, full of beer, wine and tobacco.
'B' Company lost all its officers, then its N.C.O.s, until a
Rifleman, A. E. Shepherd, the company commander's
orderly, took command, an act for which he was awarded
the V.C. 'B' Company, like the others, captured its objective, and the thirty-four survivors dug in as a battalion of
the Rifle Brigade passed through for the next phase.

The 10th Battalion of the 60th, moving forward as
support to the leading troops, found time to take out an
enemy strongpoint, capturing 200 prisoners in the process.

The next day German reaction stiffened, and it was the
turn of the 11th Battalion. Its task was to take the village
of Crèvecœur, which was about half-way between the
Hindenburg Line and Cambrai. The battle was now out in
the open and objectives were bridges and châteaux, not
trench lines.

The battalions got troops across the canal that protected
the town, but at last light they were withdrawn to better
positions; the attack on their left had not made progress.
For the next few days the Third Army strove to consoli-
date their gains; all thought of a cavalry breakthrough had
been abandoned. Byng's forces had nevertheless achieved
much and as church bells were pealing the victory in
England, the victors counted up the booty. Over 10,000
prisoners had been taken, nearly 300 machine-guns, and
200 guns and mortars.

This was a breach in the line that the Germans could not tolerate. On November 30, ten days after the attack began, they launched powerful counter-attacks on the bases of the salient. With tired troops and hastily dug defences, the British could not hope to hold out against such force. The troops that had gone farthest found themselves threatened from the rear and were forced to conduct fighting withdrawals. Not all got away; the 11th Battalion lost ten officers and 296 other ranks as prisoners-of-war. The 12th, after a brilliant defence of its position, was also pulled back and by December 3 both units were back in the old British front lines. The 1st Battalion, which had been operating on the left flank with the 2nd Division, and had taken part in the capture of Bourlon Wood, defended its gains with great skill until sheer superiority of force demanded a withdrawal.

Byng felt the failure deeply. It is on record that he told senior Canadian officers afterwards that his own plan had been altered beyond recognition by G.H.Q. Artillery support for the later stages had not been provided, promised reserves had not appeared. There is no reason to doubt this; the same sort of thing had been happening year after year.

Thus, as 1917 ended, the Allies held victory in their hands, for they had found the answers to all the vexing problems that had plagued them for three years. The wire could now be cut, the enemy front could now be pierced, the enemy superiority in machine-guns and artillery had been eliminated. There was every reason to suppose that a properly mounted attack, with reserves near at hand for exploitation, would win the war. Instead, 1918 very nearly ended in disaster.

The German attack, which sent the British Army reeling backwards over the ground they had captured at such cost, began in March. The Regimental Historian of this period of the 60th history is inclined to put the blame for it on a

Government that held back reserves of troops. He ignores
the distrust with which the Cabinet viewed Douglas Haig.
In any event, the 120,000 reserves retained in England
were kept there by a War Office decision and not a
deliberate Cabinet move. The policy in early 1918 was to
keep to the defensive until American strength could make
itself felt, and the troops who were not needed in the line
were better off in the comfort (what there was of it) of
England.

March 21, 1918 will always be remembered as a black
day by those in the Fifth and Third Armies who suffered
its impact. The Germans, reinforced by divisions released
from the Eastern front by the collapse of Russia, attacked
along a fifty-mile front on a foggy morning after a short

*HRH The Duke of Connaught inspects the 2nd Bn of the 60th at La
Buissiere in France on July 1st, 1918.*

but violent artillery bombardment. Infiltrating between known concentrations of troops and ignoring their flanks, the leading elements were soon shooting up gun lines and camps while successive waves dealt with the by-passed infantry. The speed of the advance, together with the unique method, threw the British line into confusion. The 14th Division, holding front-line positions near the right flank of the Fifth Army, had three battalions of the K.R.R.C.—the 7th, 8th and 9th. All three were wiped out. Battalion and even Brigade Headquarters were surrounded and dispatched at leisure while the eager infiltrators plunged on. Communications were severed everywhere. No one knew what was happening.

For once, someone was doing some clever fighting and it is a pity that it was the enemy. A survivor of the 8th Battalion, writing later, says:

> . . . about four p.m. they brought up two tanks—much larger and faster than ours—and took Calvair. After a pause the tanks came on against Louvois and proceeded to trample down the wire and shoot into the trenches . . . there were no Germans to shoot at, as they all lay low and let the tanks do the job. Under these circumstances we had no other course than to give in.

One gets the feeling from this that the writer considers it unsporting to 'let the tanks do the job'. To what low ebb had the doctrines of Bouquet and de Rothenburg fallen! The enemy, in fact, were fighting like Riflemen of the old school and it was working all too well. An officer of the 9th Battalion who was captured said: '. . . when taken to their Brigade Headquarters, we found it already established behind us, on the way to our old Brigade Headquarters.'

The 17th Battalion, away to the Fifth Army's left flank, went through a similar experience but managed to retain its identity, though suffering severe casualties.

The preoccupation with 'holding a line' had given the enemy this chance although it took three years for them to realize it. In the end, their own courage failed them and they tried to maintain the ground they had won by establishing a line. After that, the Allied superiority in manpower made itself felt and the great advance was contained and slowed. The 11th and 12th Battalions of the 60th participated in these later operations, suffering cruelly from a disorganized artillery support, scanty rations, and an inadequate supply of ammunition. The regimental historian records their fate: 'These two battalions, though in and out of the trenches till the Armistice, took no part in any more great operations.'

The 1st Battalion was still in the 2nd Division, and helped to form the pivot of the Third Army as it swung back to conform with the Fifth's withdrawal. More than once reduced to less than a company, it fought back as reinforcements arrived; but the rearguard actions were trying as, on March 26, it found itself reoccupying the old British trenches from which the Somme battles had begun. 'The position was a fairly good one,' recorded their C.O., 'as the old trenches had stood the weather wonderfully well.'

As if this were not enough participation by one regiment in a debacle, the 18th got mixed up in it. Just returned from Italy after a year's quiet soldiering with the 41st Division, the 18th became involved in the March battles while the German attack was still rolling and was all but eliminated as a fighting force after only a few days of desperate fighting. The regimental *Chronicle* sums up its traumatic experience: 'Thus ended an eventful month. Our fine Battalion of nearly 900 other ranks had been reduced to about 80.'

On April 9, on the anniversary of the capture of Vimy Ridge, the Germans attacked the Ypres salient, and three days later had eliminated the British gains at Passchendaele. In the process the offensive all but eliminated the 16th Battalion which fought on for three days after it had been surrounded and cut off. But the overall gains were getting smaller as resistance stiffened with the arrival of new troops from England. The enemy had poured all his resources into the great attack, but it had not been enough. The line was stabilized, the regiments were replenished and on July 18 General Foch, now Commander-in-Chief of all the Allied armies, began counter-attacks with the French Army that were to lead to victory, aided by an influenza epidemic that struck harder at the under-nourished German soldiers than the Allies.

Three weeks later, on August 8, the British armies joined in, attacking the great bulge that the German offensive had made in the line. From the first, the operations were successful. It was as if the High Command, having survived the worst the enemy could do, had acquired a new lease of life. So had the troops. They marched and fought like new men, for the trenches were soon left behind and mobile war again provided challenge and change. The casualties were lighter too, and men survived from attack to attack, while their units readily absorbed the comparatively few reinforcements that were needed. The Allies got better and better as the weeks passed, while their desperate enemy, who had used the last of his reserves, weakened steadily.

Five battalions of the 60th participated in this last phase of the First World War. The 4th Battalion, newly returned from two years of stationary warfare at Salonika, seemed to revel in the new war of movement as it captured each objective assigned to it by the 50th Division. The others, old names by now, with new faces, the 1st and 2nd, the 13th and 16th, remembered the old skills as the advance swept on towards the Rhine. The pace was still infantry pace; fast tanks were for the next war. But each day recorded new successes and, by the end of the first week in November, one could see the finish of it. The last units in action, the gallant 16th, and the new boys of the 4th, were together for the last stages of the pursuit, though in different divisions. The end came on November 11.

The K.R.R.C. learned little that was new in the First World War. One is so accustomed to expect technical advances during war, that it is startling to realize how little the infantry in general and the Rifles in particular departed from tradition. In fact, much that the Riflemen had learned about fighting was put aside for the 'trench warfare' period.

The British fought, for the most part, with the weapons used in the South African War. The tank and the aeroplane appeared, it is true, but their possibilities were never exploited in the First World War. The troops ended the war with the same rifle they had on its outbreak. The capabilities of the machine-gun and the use of concentrated artillery fire were developed and improved, poison gas was tried and its limitations realized, but 'fire and movement' on the battlefield was all but forgotten except on trench raids. One can say, with some accuracy, that the infantry of the line learned to fight like riflemen, while riflemen were forced to fight like the rest. The priceless benefit of mobility was largely denied them.

Many 60th officers achieved high rank and the Regiment turned out two Lieutenant-Generals, 12 Major-Generals

An experimental mechanized machine gun Company of the 2nd Bn, The 60th at Aldershot in 1928.

and 27 Brigadier-Generals. Eight members of the Regiment were awarded the Victoria Cross, helping to win its 71 battle honours. Its 12,824 dead did their part, too, and their names are emblazoned in Winchester Cathedral in perpetual memory.

Chapter 7

Praise God, now, for an English war—
The grey tide and the sullen coast,
The menace of the urgent hour,
The single island, like a tower,
Ringed with an angry host.

DOROTHY L. SAYERS

THERE HAD BEEN many small units and groups of
the K.R.R.C. serving around the world in the First
World War; in Murmansk, in North Russia, a
company from the Regiment was fighting Bolsheviks until
the spring of 1919. But by the end of that year the wartime
army was back home and all the 'New Army' battalions
had been disbanded. The Regulars were soon back at
garrison duty, the 1st and 2nd Battalions in Ireland, the
3rd and 4th in India. The latter two did not remain long.
The usual post-war economies prompted their disbandment, after a history that covered three decades. The 1st
left Ireland to take their place.

There were many more moves of this sort in the next
twenty years, to Germany, Palestine, Waziristan, Burma
and Egypt. Clashes with tribal insurgents and rebellious
nationals did not require much in the way of new weapons
and few innovations were made. Wartime stocks had to
be used up first, in any case.

It was different at home, where the authorities gradually
became aware of Germany's new armies. As a result of
Hitler's success at absorbing a large part of Europe by a
series of bloodless coups, and during the breathing-space
after Munich, a more realistic British approach to the

likelihood of war emerged, which had far-reaching effects on the 60th; the menace of German armour forced a modernization programme. The Regiment (and the Rifle Brigade) was converted into a number of Motor Battalions, each equipped with a well-developed signals network and designed to fight in co-operation with armoured formations. The 60th role as innovator was invoked again with the development of reconnaissance platoons and with the change from reliance on horses and mules to the use of the vastly quicker, if initially less reliable, mechanized first-line transport system. As new and better weapons and equipment became available, the Regiment's battalions became truly formidable fighting machines.

The fortunes of war, however, decreed that the first Riflemen into action in the Second World War found themselves fighting a defensive battle, against great odds, without much of their new equipment. The battle honour 'Calais', earned in the dark days of 1940, is held by few: a British brigade group, in fact, of which two battalions were from The King's Royal Rifle Corps.

The fall of France was imminent when the K.R.R.C. were sent to take part; German tanks were slicing through the French armies at will. One thrust, coming up from Abbeville, was charged with getting behind the B.E.F. and capturing the Channel ports, thus cutting its communications and sealing off its retirement routes. The British Government decided to slow down this dangerous advance by operating against its flanks and sent to Calais the most mobile and heavily armoured force at its disposal. The infantry were motorized in one way or another; the 2nd Battalion, K.R.R.C. was equipped with carriers, trucks, machine-guns and mortars and the 1st Queen Victoria's Rifles (7th K.R.R.C.) was a well-armed motor-cycle unit. The Rifle Brigade sent its motorized 1st Battalion and the Royal Tank Regiment its 3rd Battalion. An anti-tank battery, Royal Artillery, rounded off the organization.

By May 23, all this force (called the 30th Infantry Brigade) had landed at Calais. Troubles began at once. Not only was the town crowded with unarmed French soldiers but the dock workers, worn out with days of unloading, refused to unload the ship carrying most of the transport and ammunition of the 1st Rifle Brigade. The Queen Victoria's Rifles were sent without transport of any sort; it was to form a firm base at Calais from which the rest of the force would sally out against the Panzer columns.

Unfortunately, the Panzer columns were already there, blocking the road to Dunkirk. An immediate sortie, aimed at getting food and ammunition through to the B.E.F., bumped into strong tank forces on the coastal road and, although one squadron of British armour got through, the rest of the force was turned back. There was just time to form a thin defence perimeter around the city, along the ancient ramparts, when the enemy arrived in strength and began to attack.

The Queen Victoria's Rifles had been given the outpost role and, on May 23, the enemy probed their hastily prepared positions, while registering mortars on targets in the city. There was no British field artillery to engage these mortars and they fired without interference throughout the action that followed. The next day, at first light, a platoon of D Company was the first of the Calais garrison to be treated to the new German methods of attack.

> About half a platoon of German infantry was sighted and, when fired upon, at once went to ground. After about half an hour, the enemy opened mortar fire, killing two riflemen and wounding two others . . . Soon afterwards two German light tanks approached the roadblock.

The outpost knocked out both of them with anti-tank rifles and was withdrawn to the rampart positions. So, too, were the other outposts; their task, of giving warning of an attack, had been accomplished. The brigade braced itself and awaited siege.

The German attack was not long in coming. As mortar and gunfire increased, the defenders on the ramparts could see parties of Germans working their way forward in rushes, ignoring casualties. Several of these parties were flung back by patrols that went out and engaged them at close range. But these attacks were made by the 2nd Battalion's slim reserves and could not long continue. The enemy pressure increased, aided by heavier tanks and accurate shelling. Casualties among the defenders grew steadily. Evening came and with it the knowledge that the perimeter could not be held for another day. All the main assaults had been repelled, but small groups had infiltrated the thin lines of defence and were soon firing from houses in the rear.

During the night the Riflemen were ordered back to inner defence positions, defined by the old city and protected by a canal. Thankfully, the enemy decided to wait for daylight to follow. There was time for food and replenishment of ammunition. But there was little sleep, and the brigade had not had much of that commodity since leaving England.

In the morning the battle began again, as the enemy moved into Calais in strength and attacked the remnants of the 30th Brigade. During the fighting, the troops were told that there was to be no evacuation; they were to hold Calais as long as they could. By keeping a large enemy force engaged, they were weakening the effort that could be brought against the Dunkirk defences, and it was through Dunkirk, and only Dunkirk, that the B.E.F. could escape.

The decision had been taken by the Prime Minister himself. Lord Ismay has recorded the circumstances in his memoirs:

The decision affected all of us very deeply, especially perhaps Churchill. He was unusually silent during dinner that evening, and he ate and drank with evident distaste. As we rose from the table he said, 'I feel physically sick.' He has quoted these words in his memoirs, but he does not mention how sad he looked as he uttered them.

The Battle of Calais, 1940, ended the next afternoon. With their ranks thinned by casualties and no guns with which to reply to the incessant shelling, the surviving Riflemen were fighting off the 10th Division of Guderian's Panzer Corps. Much of the city was in flames and communications had been sundered. About 4 p.m., after a quick check of the remaining position, the C.O. of the

In 1945 Major General (later General) Sir George Erskine unveiled a memorial to those members of the 60th, the Rifle Brigade and The Queen Victoria Rifles who fell in the Defence of Calais.

105

2nd Battalion ordered the survivors of the two K.R.R.C. units to disperse until dark amid the burning buildings, and then try to escape. None did, though some died trying. Later on, during the march to German P.O.W. camps, four officers and two other ranks did escape.

In the House of Commons Mr. Churchill, in paying tribute to the gallantry of the defenders, said, 'Thus it was that the port of Dunkirk was kept open.' King George VI, the Colonel-in-Chief of the 60th, said that the defence of Calais was in keeping with the highest traditions of the regiment and marked 'a glorious page in its history'.

Back in England, steps were taken to rebuild the two battalions. In the meantime, the 1st, in far-away North Africa, was doing its share of adding to the laurels of the Regiment. It had been in Egypt since the end of 1938, commanded by Lieutenant-Colonel William Henry Ewart Gott, M.C. Gott had been a lieutenant in the First World War, and had climbed the slow peacetime ladder of promotion to command of his battalion. Within three years of the outbreak of war he was a Lieutenant-General, and Churchill's nominee for command of the Eighth Army. His untimely and much lamented death (his aircraft was shot down near Cairo on the eve of his last great appointment) ended prematurely a brilliant career. He had been largely responsible for developing Motor Battalion theories and, although he never actually commanded a battalion of the 60th in battle, his training of the 1st Battalion was a major factor in its subsequent successes in the Desert War; when the Italians declared war in 1940 he had just been made G.S.O.1 of the Middle East's only Armoured Division.

The Italian army in Libya seemed to possess the initiative; it outnumbered by far the British Army in Egypt. But the 1st Battalion struck a shrewd blow that presaged future operations in the area when, a few days after the Italian declaration of war, 'D' Company, with tank sup-

Lieutenant-General 'Strafer' Gott

port, reduced the border strong-point of Fort Capuzzo to a flaming ruin, capturing over 200 prisoners.

After that, there were months of raids and patrols as, trained for desert warfare, the Riflemen did pretty much as they pleased with the Italians they came across. This period brought reorganizations, forced by the experience in North-West Europe. The 1st Battalion became part of a Support Group, an early development in the organization of armoured divisions. With it were the 2nd Battalion of the Rifle Brigade and the 4th Regiment, Royal Horse Artillery. Needless to say, there were no horses. In September this Group, which had been observing enemy movements, discovered that the Italians were slowly advancing along the coast. A series of fighting rearguard actions followed which ended at Sidi Barrani, well inside the Egyptian border. In the words of one observer, 'the enemy . . . evidently considered he had gone far enough when he had attacked and valiantly captured the empty and undefended village'.

This cautious forward move of the Italian army set the scene for its destruction. Its lines of communication were now stretched to their limits, and its camps and bivouacs spread out in a sort of battle order, designed to give comfort in the desert rather than defence against aggression. The British patrolled deeply, pinpointing each vulnerable target. The 60th were expert in this information-gathering operation, and a complete picture of the enemy dispositions was soon built up in the planning rooms of the British Desert Army.

When all was known, the Commander-in-Chief, General Wavell, launched his famous offensive, an attack by some 30,000 against an Italian army numbering in all about 250,000.

Churchill has said that the British were 'Lean, bronzed, desert-hardened and completely mechanized'. Even so, the odds were staggering. The battle began on December 9, 1940, and its progress has been told many times. The best account is by the late John Connell, who wrote: 'If numbers were all that mattered in war, Wavell had not a chance.' But quality and determination told; by December 12, three days after the assault began, four Italian divisions had been destroyed, two more were in full retreat and the Desert Army had a delicious new problem—its 40,000 prisoners. Egypt had been all but freed of the invaders and the way ahead opened invitingly.

The armoured division of which the 60th was a part waited impatiently for orders to proceed. Its role in the opening phase had been to get in behind the forward Italian forces and prevent their escape. This it had done superbly well. The 1st Battalion had protected the left flank of this move, with the rest of the Support Group.

When the order came to continue the advance, it concentrated on its classic role of following up and reporting movement as the remnants of the Italians retreated. At Bardia, and later at Tobruk, it helped form cut-off groups that netted still more prisoners.

Throughout January British victories in the desert claimed the headlines around the world. The Italian army had been utterly demoralized and the Desert Army increased the pressure. Benghazi fell on February 7, after a two-day battle against desperate Italian attempts to break the ring of vengeful desert fighters. Few got through, and General O'Connor, the field commander of the Desert Force, was able to say in his official report, 'I think this may be termed a complete victory as none of the enemy escaped'.

The 1st Battalion, held up by rough going on the flank, missed this last battle, but saw its aftermath:

> After we had gone a few miles south . . . we came upon the scene of the campaign's last great battle . . . an imposing mess of shattered Italian tanks, abandoned guns and derelict lorries. There was the familiar sight of hordes of prisoners being rounded up; processions of staff cars, containing General Bergonzoli and his entourage, passed up the road towards Benghazi.

The battalion had now been fighting in the desert for ten months; it was worn out and in need of rest. On February 28, 1941, it returned to Cairo for refit, but in six weeks it was back in action. General Erwin Rommel had arrived in North Africa. The British, over-extended and weakened by withdrawals of troops for the campaign in Greece, fell back from the thinly held positions at Agedabia, pressed by the Afrika Korps and a rejuvenated Italian army. The 1st Battalion acted as a rearguard in the ensuing retreat to the Egyptian border.

The many rearguard actions that flared up during this unhappy withdrawal make spirited reading in the Chronicles of the 60th. The morale of the 1st Battalion was, if anything, higher at the end of the long retreat than it had been at the beginning. It had fought Germans to a standstill when anything like equal numbers were involved.

The 9th Battalion (1st Battalion, The Rangers) spent this period in Greece. It had been in Egypt since late December 1940, training for desert warfare. Events in Europe changed its destination. Early in the New Year, when the decision was taken to go to the aid of the Greeks in their struggle with the Axis, the training stopped and the fighting began, in a country far different than the Libyan desert. Landing at Piraeus on March 15, the 9th became part of the 1st Armoured Brigade.

The wisdom of the decision to go to Greece has been hotly debated by military and political strategists. One thing is certain: it meant the loss of all the gains in Africa. There were not enough troops left in the desert to withstand determined counter-attack. General de Guingand, a key figure in the planning of the expedition, has said, '. . . whether it was a job worth doing and in our best interests seemed to me very doubtful'.

The 9th Battalion would have agreed with him. Harried from the defensive line it had helped to build, fighting dogged rearguard actions (the Florina Gap was an outstanding example), with no air-cover and not enough artillery, many Riflemen must have wondered just what it was they were supposed to be accomplishing. By April 27 the depleted battalion had been evacuated across the beaches at Rafina, near Athens. It had been in Greece just six weeks.

But the trials of the Greek intervention were not over; in fact, they had just begun. A small portion of the 9th was shipped direct to Egypt, but most of it found itself in Crete. The less said about this decision the better. It had been taken hastily, in the face of shortages of every type of equipment from munitions to mess tins. The inevitable attack by air and sea, when it came, was splendidly frustrated for many days, so much so that Germany never again attempted airborne landings, but the end was never in doubt. The defending forces were gradually cut up and isolated. Thereafter, it was a march across the island to the southern shore, where, early on June 1, a handful of the 9th was taken off by a destroyer fortunate enough to escape dive-bombing. The remainder went into prisoner-of-war camps.

Much had happened in the desert during the short campaign in Greece. The British had stopped Rommel at Sollum, while establishing a strong garrison at Tobruk to threaten the enemy lines of communications. In May, and again in June, the Desert Army had gone over to the attack, attempting to link up with Tobruk. These ventures had been unsuccessful and both sides had paused to reinforce and re-equip.

In September the 1st Battalion, deployed in outpost positions, helped to defeat an assault designed by Rommel to test the defences facing him. Indecisive war went on until November, when Auchinleck took over from Wavell and, with a well-rested army, commanded now by Lieutenant-General N. M. Ritchie, began a massive effort to drive the Germans and Italians back. 'Strafer' Gott was by now commanding the 7th Armoured Division and his old battalion, the 1st, was under his command, in the Divisional Support Group. The immediate aim was the relief of Tobruk; the ultimate—the defeat of the Afrika Korps.

This first serious attempt to oust Rommel from North Africa soon became a swaying, shifting battle that had no precedent in military history. Armoured columns dashed at each other in contact battles obscured by clouds of dust and sand. In such confusion, communications became all important; loss of control by commanders meant defeat in detail.

This almost happened to the Desert Army; John Connell has said of it that 'it was a strange bewildering battle to fight . . . the original plan . . . broke up rapidly and totally'. For the first few days the fighting swirled around Sidi Rezegh airfield, a key to the relief of Tobruk. Here the 1st Battalion contributed an epic fight to the 60th's history. The 6th Royal Tank Regiment had plunged through to the airfield and on November 20 the 1st Battalion had driven across country to join it. Early next morning it was ordered to attack the escarpment north of the airfield, possession of which would give observation over the enemy-held road to Tobruk. Without tank support (the 6th R.T.R. were already heavily engaged), the battalion lined up for the long dash to the height. The Commanding Officer, Lieutenant-Colonel S. C. F. de Salis, 'walked along the line of companies wishing everyone good luck'. Then the artillery barrage came down, the carriers rolled forward from behind the waiting motor platoons, and the C.O. signalled the advance.

The Riflemen on foot, advancing in extended order, found themselves attacking enemy positions that had by no means been subdued by the carrier attack. The defence proved to be far more formidable than had been estimated. Five of 'D' Company's seven carriers had been quickly put out of action and the platoon commander killed. The other carrier platoons had suffered too. The enemy had adopted Wellingtonian tactics, siting their main force on the reverse slope of the escarpment. The advancing Riflemen found themselves in the role of Wellington's French enemy. Unlike the French, they had an effective alternative to massive advance in column. Breaking at once into small battle groups, they closed with the enemy using 'fire and movement', one group covering the movement forward of the next, until the moment came to charge the enemy position. Rifleman J. Beeley, firing his Bren gun from the hip, accounted for a seven-man crew manning an anti-tank

112

gun and a machine-gun before falling within twenty yards of the enemy position. He was awarded a posthumous Victoria Cross.

By using these tactics with dash and persistence, the 1st Battalion had a firm hold on the escarpment by noon. It had driven off about 1,000 of the enemy, inflicted many casualties, and captured 700 prisoners. Eight 60th officers and 76 other ranks were killed or wounded. It had been a textbook operation, in which superb training had cancelled out the odds.

The 1st Battalion was not left long in possession of the escarpment. As artillery observation posts came forward to the ridge and began to bring down fire on the road to Tobruk, the enemy marshalled to regain the position; it was too valuable to leave in British hands. After a day in possession, the 60th was heavily shelled and in the early afternoon a massive attack was launched, led by about 80 tanks. With no tanks of their own to lend aid, and only two 2-pounder anti-tank guns, the Riflemen were simply overwhelmed. By the time British tanks did appear, the infantry battle was over. Remnants of the battalion remained hidden until darkness and regained the British lines but the C.O. and most of the survivors were taken prisoner.

The work of reconstituting the Battalion began at once.

The story of the rest of the campaign has been told before. The British, by persisting with their offensive in spite of every indication that they had lost the initiative, fought Rommel into retreat and followed him as far west as El Agheila. There, the familiar pattern was repeated; with a supply line 1,000 miles long, the exhausted pursuers could not defend their gains. On January 21, 1942, Rommel attacked again with fresh troops. This time the 2nd Battalion of the 60th, as part of the 1st Armoured Division, participated in the retreat. It ended at Gazala, a half-way point, where the German advance was halted and contained.

The armament of motor battalions had steadily improved as new weapons became available. In place of the 1st Battalion's handful of 2-pounder guns, the 2nd had sixteen 6-pounders which, with medium machine-guns and 3-inch mortars, provided a welcome increase of readily available fire-power. The next tangle with the Afrika Korps was anticipated with confidence.

The 1st Battalion was ready for action again in March 1942 and rejoined the 7th Armoured Division in a reserve position behind the forward lines. The 9th, reconstituted after its experience in Greece and Crete, was ready in April, and, shortly afterwards, moved westward across the desert to help occupy the Gazala positions. There were thus three battalions of the Regiment in the Desert Army as spring came to 1942. The Eighth Army, as it was now called, had elected to remain on the defensive for the next battle, hoping to destroy the enemy on ground it had prepared for counter-attack.

Chapter 8

What did I see in the desert today,
In the cold, pale light of dawn?
I saw the Honeys creaking out,
Their brave, bright pennants torn;
And heads were high against the sky,
And faces were grim and drawn.

BOMBARDIER L. CHALLONER

THE NEXT PHASE of the desert fighting—the summer battles of 1942—found all three battalions of the K.R.R.C. awaiting attack on the Gazala–Bir Hacheim Line. The 1st was with the 7th Armoured Division, the 2nd with the 1st Armoured Division, and the 9th was in reserve, relieving the other two for rest out of the line.

During this period the 'Jock Columns' came into their own. Named after Brigadier Jock Campbell, the commander of the 7th Armoured Division's Support group, they were small columns of all arms containing one or more motor companies. Their role was long-range reconnaissance while harrying the enemy. Hiding in wadis during the day, they would emerge at dusk or dawn, shoot up supply columns or careless troops, leave blazing vehicles as a visiting card, and roar away into the desert before the enemy could react. Eighth Army relied heavily on the intimate, day-to-day reports which such activity produced. The Jock Columns were the cavalry of the desert; those who participated (and the K.R.R.C. were constantly involved) will always remember it as an exhilarating and somewhat dangerous experience.

The British defences at Gazala were designed to permit

enemy penetration between defended localities into what was hoped would become 'killing grounds' where British armour could destroy the enemy armour, cut off by the defended localities from their supplies and reserves. Such a defence, admirable in theory, presupposed that the localities could be properly defended. In fact, many were not, as the 9th Battalion found when, on the night of May 25, 1942, it relieved the 2nd in the locality known as 'the Rhetima Box', near Bir Hacheim. About four miles square, it was 'marked by a single wire laid on the ground'. All the approaches could not be covered with fire and it was overlooked in several places by higher ground. Many of the weapon positions had not been properly prepared for defence and communications were inadequate. There was, however, a minefield around it.

The next afternoon, with the sun behind him, Rommel attacked. The Rhetima Box was quite unable to withstand the massive tank assault and broke up. Two companies of the 9th were overrun and the survivors taken prisoner. The rest of the Battalion joined the remainder of the garrison in rapid withdrawal. All the battalion carriers and the administrative vehicles were lost.

The 1st Battalion was also near Bir Hacheim, in reserve. With news of the German attack came orders to be ready to join 4th Armoured Brigade, under whose command it was to operate. The formal divisional organization had been ignored in the desert at this time: smaller and more flexible formations were thought to be better and the brigade group of all arms was the rule. This dispersion of force was to prove costly in the days that followed.

At 7.30 a.m. on May 28, 100 German tanks burst out over the skyline, surprising the whole 4th Armoured Brigade. The desperate battle that followed also broke up this formation into scattered groups, fighting well, but without enough punch to mount a co-ordinated counterattack. The Commanding Officer of the 1st Battalion was captured on his way to meet the Brigadier, but in the *mêlée* a message got through ordering the Battalion north to help stem Rommel's main assault. After a tremendous effort, this was accomplished; the Afrika Korps was halted, with its back against the minefields of the forward localities and its water, food and ammunition running short. But the British forces had been badly shaken by the strength of the attack and the swift counter-stroke which should have finished the campaign was never launched. While Rommel wrote to his wife about the bitter possibility of having to surrender, the staff of the Eighth Army dithered. One gets the very definite impression of an inexperienced commander penning formal appreciations on what to do next, as if on a Staff College exercise, while the chance to strike a winning blow slipped inexorably away from him.

Rommel was permitted to restock and reinforce (he led one relief column through the minefields himself), while Eighth Army churned out 'courses open to the enemy' and 'courses open to us'. As a result, when a British attack was finally launched, on June 5, in the area known as the 'Cauldron', a refreshed and invigorated Afrika Korps met and defeated it decisively. It was once again Rommel's turn, and this time there were no more 'defended localities' to channel his advance. On June 12 he attacked savagely, with all his armour, and at once made progress; the desperate British attempts to hold him were made piecemeal.

German columns were soon whipping about in the rear areas of the Eighth Army. Tobruk, too hastily garrisoned, fell into enemy hands and a general retreat to the Egyptian border followed. A 60th officer has described what it was like:

> It was the night of the full moon—a great yellow pumpkin floating about in a pale sky . . . We went east pretty fast. It was like General Post. There were British columns and German ones, cannoning off each other like blinded people. You could see the

lolloping Very lights, and like a bass string accompaniment you could hear as background to everything the grunting, coughing mumbling of the Panzers moving east.

After this, Ritchie had to go, and Auchinleck took over personal command, determined to fight a good battle for the frontier. The dispositions were Ritchie's, and there was no time to change much of them. The Eighth Army, almost bereft of tanks, was spread out far too thin; Rommel had only to choose his gap. Cairo beckoned, and Mussolini flew to North Africa to participate in the victory parade.

What followed has been called the First Battle of El Alamein and was, under the circumstances, unbelievably successful. The few changes in the defence that Auchinleck was able to make halted the tired Teutons and postponed the decision. Rommel's last attack, aimed at Ruweisat Ridge, fell upon the 4th Armoured Brigade, which still included the 1st Battalion. The Regimental History has the story:

> At this point, the Commanding Officer, 1st Royal Horse Artillery, made a decision. He announced his resolve to fight to the last with his Regiment. Lieutenant-Colonel C. d'A. P. Consett concurred on behalf of the Battalion.

The Riflemen dug themselves in a few hundred yards ahead of the field guns. All the units on the Ridge were under-strength and tired—but this was to be the last stand. Behind them lay the defenceless Delta. At dusk the assault came in, led by 20 tanks. It was driven off; some field guns were firing solid shot over open sights. The British stood to all night, but there was no further attempt. At first light on July 4, the incredulous defenders saw that the Germans had been so sure of victory that they had leaguered for the night less than 1,000 yards away.

> Immediately a tremendous barrage was put down on the sleeping Huns by the 1st Royal Horse Artillery and other batteries of

118

25-pounders which had come up. Our tanks also joined in the massacre. The Germans had to abandon whatever designs they had for 4th July.

This defiant stand, repeated elsewhere along the El Alamein 'Line', stopped Rommel's advance to Cairo. For some days he thrust at the British barrier. Then, realizing that he could go no further without reinforcement, he pulled back and, in his turn, ordered his troops to dig in. From this point onwards, the sands of time ran against the Afrika Korps.

What was left of July became a welcome breathing spell, but it carried with it misfortune. The Battalions of the K.R.R.C. were withdrawn into rest, only to hear that the 9th was to be disbanded to provide replacements for the 1st and 2nd. It was during this period that General Gott was killed when his aircraft was shot down by a German fighter.

In mid-August the Prime Minister visited the Middle East, and one result was that General Montgomery took over the Eighth Army. Alexander relieved Auchinleck as Commander-in-Chief. Two weeks later Rommel attacked again.

The Battle of Alam Halfa brought renewed self-confidence to the Eighth Army. The 13th Corps, which fought the main battle, had been Gott's; now it was under Lieutenant-General Brian Horrocks, newly arrived from Britain. Under the new dispensation, this battle was tightly controlled and never allowed to get out of hand. Rommel was encouraged, by various stratagems, to attack the British positions at the strongest point, Alam Halfa Ridge, and as he drove towards it through the minefields, he was harried by both battalions of the 60th. The 1st had a field day on Heimeimat Ridge, which marked the southern flank.

'The enemy came eastward in full strength,' wrote one of the company commanders, 'hitting our forward minefield . . . at midnight. From then on until dawn we hung on, harassing them below with machine guns and Brens from the high ground.'

During this phase of the battle, the Desert Air Force found the enemy and dropped flares. 'It was one of the most awe-inspiring sights I shall ever see . . . the whole valley with its mass of the Afrika Korps stationary was lit up like a huge orange fairyland.'

It was, in truth, no fairyland. The Afrika Korps came on with all its old dash, and away to the north the 2nd Battalion was duplicating the activity of the 1st, harassing, delaying, transmitting information. The 2nd Battalion and the Rifle Brigade were able to strike shrewd blows, but it was obvious that here was the enemy's main attack. In front of Alam Halfa Ridge it was stopped cold by British armour and artillery in prepared positions and Rommel, unable this time to tempt the British into hasty counter-attack, had to withdraw the beaten remnants of his Panzer divisions to his original starting-point.

The first round of the new Alamein battle had gone decisively to the defenders.

With Rommel repulsed, Montgomery set his sights on his own offensive, the story of which has passed into history as one of the decisive battles of the war. It began on October 23, and three battalions of the K.R.R.C. were involved, one with each Armoured Division. The 1st was with the Desert Rats (7th Armoured), the 2nd was with the 1st Armoured Division and the recently arrived 11th (the 1st Battalion The Queen's Westminsters) fought with the 10th Armoured Division. Its battle, brief and bloody, began on the opening night.

Five days later, what was left of it was pulled out of action with the rest of the Armoured Brigade of which it was a part, as survivors of the so-called 'Dog fight' phase. It was then ordered to turn over its weapons and equipment to the 2nd Battalion.

The 1st Battalion was with the Desert Rats in the south when the battle began, with the role of keeping Rommel's 21st Panzer Division occupied. When the 1st and 10th Armoured Divisions found it impossible to break clear of the minefields, a massive regrouping followed and the 7th came north. It, too, ran into the Afrika Korps' screen of anti-tank guns but the extra impetus of the shift of forces began to work when, after dark on November 2, the Motor Brigade of which the 2nd was a part, put in an attack on the anti-tank gun line. The night assault was successful, and the enemy's dawn counter-attack was repulsed. The following morning the armoured brigades, the 1st Battalion leading the 4th Light Armoured, broke out into open ground through the 2nd Battalion's position.

The war of manœuvre, dear to the hearts of Eighth

Brewing up—the 2nd Bn in the Western Desert.

Army veterans, was on again and the chronicler of the 1st Battalion echoed the jubilation:

> The breakthrough was now confirmed. The battle of Alamein was won! . . . from now on the battle would be mobile and the desert to the west was open to any manœuvre the Eighth Army chose to make . . .
>
> As the Riflemen mounted their trucks with beaming faces . . . the cry was 'On to Benghazi!'

Eight days later the Battalion was probing the enemy rearguard positions at Halfaya Pass. By November 20 it was indeed at Benghazi. By the end of the month the Army was closing up to the enemy defence line at El Agheila. It had been there twice before, but it had never got beyond. This time the administrative arrangements had been better planned. A wide outflanking movement, combined with a savage attack on the positions themselves, did the trick. Rommel, once more severely mauled, pulled back hurriedly and the Eighth Army was left in undisputed possession of all North Africa from Cairo to Tripolitania, a distance of 1,000 miles. Final victory now seemed possible.

Throughout the rest of December and into January 1943, strenuous efforts were made to bring forward stores and replacements for a further advance, an operation that permitted some rest and refit. The 1st Battalion, which had been in the van from Alamein to Agheila, went into reserve, replaced in the 4th Light Armoured Brigade by the 2nd, which had been recuperating since Alamein.

When all was ready, a series of outflanking moves began, which hustled the Afrika Korps out of one position after another until Tripoli was surrendered on January 23. The Eighth Army—and the 60th—had come a long way. Now massive, mobile and well-equipped, it swept all opposition before it. A 1st Battalion officer (the unit returned, with the 1st Armoured Division, in time to

A Rifleman of the 60th with his pet Desert Rat—Mareth 1943.

participate in the advance on Tunis) wrote at the time, 'We seldom move less than a Brigade strong, guns never fire in troops; they seem to have regimental tasks as a minimum, with divisional concentrations as the normal. Effective to judge by results, but much less fun to us, who are really more like lorry infantry these days than motor battalions.'

It was, indeed, much less fun. As the British armies grew in size and power, the war became complex. In the process of shifting great bodies of heavily-equipped troops from battle to battle, operations became almost businesslike, though the casualties continued. The excitement of small unit actions, fought on an enormous desert battleground, became a nostalgic memory. Of all the theatres in which the British fought, the desert remains most evocative, stirring the thoughts and brightening the eyes of those who survived it.

For the 60th, it was a tailor-made situation. The reconnaissance and harassing role which it had created and developed was perfect for the desert situation. The first brush with the enemy was in the regimental bloodstream, and the Jock Columns, which all battalions worked with at one time or another, were in every sense 'Swift and Bold'. Now, with the desert arena conquered, the fighting ahead was to be far less pleasant.

There was much to do before Tunis was reached and North Africa freed of Nazi soldiers. The Anglo-American forces that had landed in Algeria fought their way eastward and the 1st Battalion, as part of the 1st Armoured Division, joined them overland for the final thrust, towards Tunis.

Men of the 11th Bn setting out on a fighting patrol in Italy.

Rommel fought hard to the end, then flew home, leaving his surviving troops in prisoner-of-war cages.

After that, both battalions went into reserve and watched the invasion of Sicily from the North African shore. Their services were not called for until late in October, when the 2nd Battalion rejoined 4th Armoured Brigade for an advance up Italy's Adriatic coast. The 11th Battalion, which, after Alamein, had been serving in Syria, came in from North Africa to join the 23rd Armoured Brigade on the west coast.

By then, the Italian campaign had become a slogging match, with the Germans contesting every yard of the peninsula. The Allies justified the campaign by asserting that they were holding down German divisions which might otherwise have been used in Russia or North-West Europe. The Germans, in fact, by their stubborn defence, held down far more Allied divisions than they themselves used in Italy.

The 2nd Battalion spent only a few months in Italy; early in 1944 they were withdrawn and sent home to prepare for the landings in North-West Europe. Their last battle, crossing the Sangro River, prompted one of their company commanders to observe that, 'this part of Italy, with its rivers, steep hills and deep valleys is no country for a Motor Battalion'. Having thus dismissed the whole operation, the 2nd packed up and sailed away, leaving the 11th Battalion to make of it what it could.

The 11th did well, but no one could make them like it. One platoon commander has recalled that 'it was a static, sticky, slimy war, with more casualties than kudos and more mud than was good for morale. There were no spectacular advances, no daring Jock Columns; just sitting and waiting and getting wet.'

It was a trying experience for the desert veterans. Throughout the winter and into the spring of 1944 the Battalion held various portions of the line, patrolling, ambushing, testing the enemy defences. In June 1944, as the Second Front in France got under way, it was withdrawn from Italy and sent back to Egypt for 'a change of air'.

It was now the turn of the 1st Battalion. It had been training in North Africa under Lieutenant-Col. E. A. W. Williams, who as adjutant had served at Calais and later escaped to England in a 'requisitioned' motor-boat. Landing at Naples on May 27, it underwent a period of indoctrination into the peculiarities of fighting in Italy and then moved north to join the 9th Armoured Brigade near Perugia. It was given the task of summer—as opposed to winter—fighting. Steaming dusty days occupied by much hill climbing took some of the lustre off the dramatic Italian landscape as Lake Trasimene was passed and Cortona was captured and Arezzo taken. Nevertheless, the summer of movement was regarded with happy recollection after August, when the Riflemen were moved to the Adriatic coast south of Rimini to prepare for the attack on the Gothic Line.

The battle began on August 25. In France, away to the north, British armoured columns were starting the race through France and Belgium. The Gothic Line battles were no such 'romp'. The German delaying tactics which had made life difficult all summer on the western flank had been fought to give time for the construction of the Gothic Line: it was a strong and deep position. To breach it, the Eighth Army concentrated a force that made the old desert fighting seem a generation away. There were 1,200 tanks, 1,000 guns and ten divisions.

The 1st Battalion joined the fighting on September 4, each company moving behind the tank regiment to which it had been assigned. The main defences had been breached and there seemed to be the likelihood of a break-out towards Rimini. But the Germans had not given up and a step-by-step battle followed as each ridge (and there were many of them) was defended bitterly. The fighting was strenuous, the casualties were high, but progress was made; the Marano River was crossed, then the Ausa. The autumn rains came, turning the shallow mountain streams into raging torrents and the roads into muddy impossibilities. But the streams were crossed and the advance went on, often yard by yard. The promised 'break-through' became a bitter joke as the Marecchio was mastered and the historic Rubicon traversed.

On the 25th the whole battalion, having passed through Cesena pursuing enemy rearguards, closed up to the Ronco River and, with a squadron of armour under command, prepared to form a bridgehead across it. It was fordable by foot but not by tanks, and the attack went in without their support. This was a common experience of the Italian front at this period and the 1st Battalion reaped the inevitable whirlwind. One by one the companies were attacked by enemy infantry supported by tanks of their own and driven back into ever-shrinking bridgeheads at the river bank. Rain began again and the water level rose rapidly. It was impossible to reinforce, or to withdraw. The survivors fought it out until overwhelmed.

Included in the heavy loss of rank and file (the better part of three companies), the 1st Battalion left seven company officers on the far side of the Ronco River and 'a number of our oldest and most experienced N.C.Os'. By the third week in November the 1st Battalion was up to strength again and fought further river crossings, notably the Cosina, the Marzeno and the Lamone.

By Christmas, the Riflemen were north-west of Ravenna. The food was good, but the fighting conditions were terrible. Early in January 1945, they pushed forward with the Canadians, stood off a determined German counter-attack and then moved gratefully into reserve. It had been a difficult winter, and there were still Germans in Italy.

127

Chapter 9

There is no sanctuary for brave men,
Danger allures them as it were a sun;
What they have dared they will dare once again
And so continue till the day is done.

A. G. HERBERTSON

WHILE THE 1ST BATTALION suffered in Italy and dreamed of the delights of desert fighting, other units of the K.R.R.C. were involved in a different sort of war. The 2nd and 12th (2nd Battalion, The Queen's Westminsters) had landed in Normandy in June 1944, to fight with tank formations in their intended role of properly constituted motor battalions. The 2nd came in shortly after 'D'-Day with the 4th Armoured Brigade, and the 12th followed on June 16 with 8th Armoured Brigade.

The Second Front, as the landing in France was called (the Italian campaign had never achieved this status in world opinion), had been the subject of debate from the time of the German invasion of Russia. It took the Dieppe disaster of 1942 to silence those who clamoured for a landing before there was a chance of success. It is easier to chalk a slogan on a piece of cardboard and carry it about the city streets than it is to launch such an operation; even the 1944 invasion, when it came, hung in the balance for weeks.

The two battalions of the K.R.R.C. served in what were called Independent Armoured Brigades. These formations, unlike those in Armoured Divisions, existed to serve the infantry. They could be, and were, shifted from division to division as the need for tank support arose and, as in the

128

past, the motor companies were frequently decentralized to regiments of armour.

Their equipment was the result of trial and error over the war years. The battalions still retained their carriers, but there were many more scout cars and half-tracks. There was a tendency to pick up items like heavy American machine-guns with their big ·50 bullets on the familiar rifleman's psychology of 'let's try the other fellow's weapons'.

The landings on 'D'-Day achieved a measure of surprise that exceeded all hopes and the task of forming a secure bridgehead was quickly achieved. But Caen, a pivotal communication centre, was not immediately captured and, although the enemy attempts to foil the invasion failed, their desperate counter-attacks delayed a break-out. Both K.R.R.C. battalions were deeply engaged in the operations that followed.

The 2nd Battalion landed with the 4th Armoured Brigade in Normandy on June 9. The three motor companies were each supporting Armoured regiments who in their turn were supporting one of the three brigades of the 51st (Highland) Division. The Battalion was continually in action and took part in most of the fighting.

After the sweep through the Falaise pocket, the 2nd Battalion struggled loose from roads congested by German dead and raced to join the pursuit. Catching up with the armour at the Seine, it participated thereafter in the advance, using all its mobility, fire power and skill to outflank and outfight the German rearguards that sought to bar the path. In the words of one of the Company Commanders it was 'taking prisoners all the way', most of whom had to be left with the Resistance.

In their mad flight, the Germans had stolen every horse and every bicycle from the French villages they passed through. Life was cheap and the man, woman or child who would not hand over a bicycle immediately was shot dead. The men of the Maquis had these and a thousand other scores to settle and perhaps not all the prisoners got back to their safe cages in England; there was no way of telling.

By September 1, the Battalion was closing up to the Somme, where Riflemen had died in thousands twenty-eight years before against the same enemy. Here the Colonel (R. B. Littledale) was killed reconnoitring the riverside village of Airaines, which had been left as a strong-point by the retreating enemy. Littledale had been at Calais and had escaped from Germany via Spain. A Canadian armoured formation (the Armoured Brigade of the 4th Armoured Division) rolled up to help at this juncture and, soon after, there were British and Canadian footholds on the far bank. A rest seemed appropriate at this time, but the need to keep the enemy off-balance took precedence and the pursuit went on.

This was the warfare for which the 60th had trained for nearly 200 years—the small unit action—swift, competent, devastating. The massive battles of thousands was the preoccupation of the regiments of the Line. But the cutting-out operation, the sudden rush that overwhelmed the rearguard and captured the vital bridge, this was a 60th speciality, and none did it any better.

From the Somme to Arras took a day, to Aix-le-Château another. German resistance had all but vanished and what there was of it was by-passed. On September 5 the 4th Armoured Brigade, in a record-breaking run, crossed the Belgian border and reached Ghent, a distance of 85 miles.

Next day, isolated enemy columns sought desperately to stem the British advance but the unco-ordinated attacks were beaten back and the Battalion, aided by Belgian resistance forces, captured the vital bridge across the Scheldt at Termonde. Here the Riflemen were joined by the 44th Battalion, Royal Tank Regiment and drove on, through cheering Belgian villages, to Hamme and St.

Nicholas, where further weak German counter-attacks were smashed. On the evening of the 10th, after an unparalleled advance, the Battalion was given three days' rest.

The 12th Battalion had had a roughly similar experience. First, the slogging matches in the bridgehead, then the break-out, followed by the pursuit across north-western France into Belgium.

A company commander of the 12th Battalion, recalling one of the many moving incidents of the pursuit, remembered:

> Up the ruined street (in Conde), pushing an overladen wheelbarrow containing all his worldly possessions, stumbled a homeless Frenchman. Proudly flying from the front of the wheelbarrow was an enormous tricolour. At every truck he paused and shook hands and grinned. His house was ruined, but his soul was free.

General Horrocks has also recorded his memories of this phase of the battle. He arrived in Normandy after a lengthy hospitalization following a desperate wound in North Africa.

> The forward area in any theatre of war, the sharp end . . . is inhabited by young men with a gleam in their eye who actually do the fighting. They are comparatively few in number, and they are nearly always the same people.

The K.R.R.C. qualify for this description and the 12th Battalion accounts substantiate it. The repeated references to the same people, the same regiments of armour and artillery, as the irresistible advance swept on across France, are ample testimony. These were exhilarating days. The hot August sun persisted, the enemy were in penny packets that only resisted long enough to permit a carrier or tank charge to testify to the scope of the victory. The war seemed about to end, and the capture of the city of

Lille by a company of the 12th, supported by a squadron of tanks, in no way diminished this feeling.

'Boys well below military age festooned the business end of every weapon in sight.

' "I'm getting a bit browned off with this," said the squadron leader, but almost immediately he got a smacking kiss from a gay thing in clinging white, and two bottles of Bollinger . . .'

Horrocks came back from a short recurrence of his illness to enjoy it too. 'Who wouldn't?' he recorded. 'We were advancing on a frontage of fifty miles; Guards Armoured, 11th Armoured Divisions and 8th Armoured Brigade [including the 12th, K.R.R.C.] were scything passages through the enemy rear areas.'

On September 5, 'A' Company of the 12th helped to capture an entire German regiment which had decided it had had enough and two days later the Battalion had driven through a wildly celebrating Brussels to concentrate at Aerschot for a further advance.

But while the regimental records are full of the triumph, there was still much fighting. Officers and men lost their lives probing enemy rearguards determined to slow the pursuit and, as the operations neared Nijmegen and Arnhem, they began to succeed.

The advance had reached the colder country of Holland, where movement was restricted to the roads. The 12th Battalion was ordered to provide flank protection along the narrow corridor punched by the effort to link up with the Arnhem drop. The corridor was kept open, but not enough troops got along it to save the Arnhem bridgehead. The survivors were brought back to defensive positions around Nijmegen, and the attack was broken off. After that, winter descended, and the necessity for a spring campaign became obvious. The British armies dug in. Now leave could be had and a little sport, with occasional training periods out of the line. In this, both battalions joined.

In the winter warfare of patrols and outpost skirmishing that followed, there was only limited opportunity to use the fire-power and mobility that had been evolved in motor battalions. The armoured half-tracks, reinforced carriers, tracked flame-throwers and scout cars in which the battalions moved and fought were a far cry from the trucks of the 1940 period, and the 6-pounder anti-tank guns, medium machine-guns and mortars would have worked wonders at Calais and in the desert fighting of 1940–42.

There was a brief opportunity to use it all in January, when the 12th Battalion accompanied the 8th Armoured Brigade in a subsidiary operation designed to close up to the Roer River. The 2nd Battalion watched the end of this attack from their front-line positions on the Maas River. Looming up for both units were the last great battles of the war, the Reichswald and Hochwald struggles.

This assault by 21st Army Group to push the Germans back to the Rhine began and ended in mud and misery. The Germans *were* pushed back, but fought hard every foot of the way; their shellfire was the heaviest of the war. Both units of the K.R.R.C. did service as line battalions, accompanying the tanks across the rain-soaked wintry fields. There were moments of wry humour towards the end, when the enemy resolution faltered. One 12th Battalion officer has written of an unexpected encounter with American tanks, moving up from the south:

> Rifleman Crossman, who was not dressy by nature and was soiled by three days and nights in action, said a few words to mark the occasion. 'So you ain't washed neither,' he observed in sour Virginian to the negro commander of the leading tank.

It took a month to 'close up to the Rhine' and the next step was obviously to cross it. The Americans were already over, miles to the south at Remagen, the weather was improving, and the end of the war could be sensed. On March 30 the 12th Battalion was across and ready for action. The 2nd had crossed five days earlier. Both were, as usual, attached to armoured formations, and with winter behind them there was the likelihood of some fast action. It came swiftly and boldly. 'The order of march appeared to be the Brigadier leading, with a liaison officer to sign the route, followed by the two commanding officers, hotly pursued by the Light Tank Reconnaissance Troop.'

The 12th had some of this, including a stiff battle for a crossing over the Twenthe Canal on April 2 that disclosed a few German teeth still biting. But with the whole country criss-crossed with advancing Allied columns, the end was in sight. The 12th, now acting as flank guard, accompanied the spearhead aimed at Bremen, while the 2nd, nodding politely as it swept past, drove on down the road to Hamburg.

There was more fierce fighting to come, as isolated German units sprang up from nowhere to defend bridges and defiles, but the end came with a cease-fire on May 5 and the famous surrender on Lüneburg Heath three days later.

In Italy, the 1st Battalion, having survived the winter of 1944–45, took stock. One officer wrote: 'There was no great climax . . . All the V-days passed us by.' The Battalion had come out of the line at the end of February, and saw no action until mid-April when the last Italian battles began. At first it was, as usual, a matter of slogging work by the infantry but, by April 19, the German defences about the Argenta Gap were crumbling and the motor companies of the 1st Battalion, each attached to a squadron of armour, attempted a break-out towards the Po. It took hard, farm-to-farm fighting, but by the 22nd the pace of the advance quickened and the battle became a matter of dislodging enemy rearguards retreating around the northern rim of the Adriatic towards Austria.

On the 23rd the Commanding Officer, Lieutenant-Colonel J. C. Hope, was mortally wounded by a sniper, a heart-breaking event with the end of the war so near. He had been a company commander in much of the desert fighting, where he was wounded, and was with the battalion when it landed in Italy. Now, as the surviving Germans began surrendering in droves amid scenes of carnage reminiscent of the Falaise Gap, the battalion mourned his loss and felt little elation at the victory. On May 3 came the cease-fire.

Soon after, the Battalion found itself in what must have been the most confusing situation of the war. As the columns drove towards Austria, partisans, slave workers, Croats, Chetniks and Titoites plugged the roads looking for revenge and loot. Few knew what their exact status was, least of all the various nationalities themselves. The most bizarre group, encountered just inside Austria, at Volkermarkt, was a 40,000-man corps of Cossack cavalry which had been fighting on the German side. The Yugo-slav partisans were particularly anxious to see their blood, and the motor platoons sought desperately to avert a minor war between them. By May 22 Marshal Tito regained some sort of control over his troops and they withdrew from Austria, much to everyone's relief. The subsequent operation designed to gather all the disparate elements into controllable camps was more exhausting than many battles.

Summer came, and the administrative pressures lessened. By September, a reorganized Battalion was back in Italy, awaiting further orders.

The 11th Battalion, after nearly a year's service in Italy, had been returned to Egypt in June 1944. But its participation in the War and its aftermath was by no means over. Sent to Greece in October to help supervise the 'liberation', the Riflemen found the Germans gone, having left chaos behind them. The British role as custodians of law and order soon became unworkable as armed bands of various political beliefs took over the countryside and began to fight it out in Athens. The Battalion withdrew from its mission of mercy in the hinterland and took on the task of participating in a civil war. The fighting was desperate and dirty.

> Lieutenant B. E. D. Collier ordered a Rifleman to fire at a young woman approaching his house with a tray of food and wine. The Rifleman obeyed and then begged not to be given such an order again. He quickly changed his view when the German stick grenade in her right hand was pointed out to him.

The battle for Athens swayed back and forth for nearly two weeks. Heavy casualties were inflicted on the insurgents, but the British were losing men too, and were too small a force to hold their ground. The situation was

Men of the 11th Bn K.R.R.C. waiting to leave H.M.S. Black Prince to land in Greece in 1944.

very grave until a British Division arrived as reinforcement and the initiative passed to the defenders. By the end of the first week in January 1945, Athens had been cleared of insurgents and British troops moved into the countryside to have another try at restoring law and order. This they speedily accomplished. The insurgents had gone to ground to await another opportunity.

Six officers and 56 other ranks were killed or wounded in the Greek Civil War of 1944–45. One officer and 83 other ranks became prisoners of the insurgents, but most of these were later released unharmed.

Thus the Second World War came to a shuddering halt for one after another of the battalions of The King's Royal Rifle Corps. The Japanese surrender and the subsequent liberation of much of South-East Asia involved the Riflemen not at all. The 11th stayed on in occupation of Greece until 1946, when it was disbanded. The 12th suffered a like fate, about the same time, after a similar post-war period of occupation in Germany.

The 1st and 2nd Battalions were part of the Regular Army. As 1946, with all its post-war disturbances, advanced, these two awaited with interest whatever tasks awaited them, deeply conscious of their heritage of danger and triumph shared. Once again the men of the 60th had been innovators, developing a mobility and a killing power never before equalled by foot soldiers. And if the past was any indication, the future would be full of challenge.

Chapter 10

War lays a burden on the reeling state,
And peace does nothing to relieve the weight.
WILLIAM COWPER

THE END OF the Second World War brought the usual reductions in military manpower that come with peace; no nation could endure for ever the burden placed on Britain's strength by the numbers in uniform in 1945. The post-war commitments that remained were studied under a microscope in an effort to reduce military expenditure and release to civilian employment the maximum number of sailors, soldiers and airmen.

The K.R.R.C. suffered along with the rest. By the end of 1946, as we have seen, the 11th and 12th Battalions had been run down. The 2nd lingered on until 1948, seemingly secure in its long history as a part of the Regular Army. It had come as no surprise when the Battalion was moved to Tripolitania in October 1945. These little strategic moves (in this case to keep the peace while the fate of the country was decided) were part of peace-time soldiering and there was scarcely a raised eyebrow when the Battalion learned that it was virtually the only British unit in the country.

It had its hands full to overflowing within a month when an Arab attack on Jewish residents of Tripoli broke out without warning. It took two weeks to restore order; there was much loss of life and damage done. But it would have been far worse if the 2nd Battalion had not been there. The Arabs faded away into the alleys and back-streets when confronted with a force with which they had no quarrel.

There were no more major outbreaks and in October

1946, after a year in Tripolitania, the 2nd Battalion moved to Palestine and was once more equipped as a motor battalion.

Here the Riflemen found themselves under an old 60th officer, Lieutenant-General Sir Evelyn Barker, who had commanded the 2nd Battalion from 1936 to 1938, a command which itself included a year in Palestine. Built in the Monty manner, lean, sharp-faced and somewhat eccentric, his sense of humour and his professional skill had become part of the lore of the 60th. In the Palestine of 1946 he and the 60th faced a terribly difficult situation. The Arabs and Jews were at each other's throats and raged at all British attempts to restore an atmosphere of law and order. Shiploads of displaced Jews, looking to Palestine as a 'homeland', swarmed into the area and all attempts to regulate the challenge were greeted with charges of anti-Semitism. To the Arab, the threat was to 'their' homeland. They felt themselves threatened with a tide of immigrants who would inevitably prove hostile. The attempt to be neutral, with the tiny country seething with unrest, imposed a heavy burden on the soldiers, and it is not to be wondered at that Britain, tiring of the role of whipping-boy, pulled out towards the end of 1947, leaving the United Nations to solve the problem.

At the request of the United Nations, however, British troops stayed on until early in 1948, when a gradual withdrawal began. The 2nd Battalion was in Palestine until the last, roaming the countryside in small armoured columns, aided from the air by light artillery observation aircraft. Finally, in May, with Arab, Egyptian and Jewish units forming up to fight the issue to a finish, the 2nd came out, to the peace and quiet of Canal Zone barracks.

In Egypt, news came that disbandment had at last been ordered, and in England, at Barton Stacey, on September 11, 1948 the 2nd Battalion ceased to exist, its Regular members transferring to the 1st Battalion.

139

While the trouble in Palestine had raged on, a whole new concept of peacetime soldiering had been worked out and implemented at home. National Service had been introduced, the cadre of Regulars had been cut to the number required to command and train the short-term conscripts, and the 1st Battalion of the 60th had been drawn into a new formation called the Green Jackets Brigade, where each battalion would, in turn, train reinforcements for the other.

This lasted for two years, when crisis in Europe and the outbreak of the war in Korea forced an augmentation of the Army; the menace was real and many of the carefully planned economies had to be abandoned. This meant, for the 60th, the end of its training role. The Depot at Winchester was set up once again and the K.R.R.C. component of the Green Jackets Brigade began jubilantly to prepare for active service.

At the same time the 2nd Battalion, so recently disbanded, made its appearance once again on the Order of Battle, the officers and men being provided equally by the 60th and The Rifle Brigade—a most happy and successful experiment. Both units became Motor Battalions in Armoured Divisions and both were sent to serve in Germany in the British Army of the Rhine.

In 1953, Coronation Year, Queen Elizabeth II assumed the appointment of Colonel-in-Chief of the 60th, following the precedent set by her father and grandfather. It was an honour deeply appreciated by all ranks of the 60th, and the successful scaling of Mount Everest by John Hunt's party (he had commanded the 11th Battalion in Italy) seemed to the 60th to be a fitting event to begin the new Elizabethan era.

The 1st Battalion remained four years in Germany, training constantly for its role of 'deterring aggression'. Then, in 1955, a change of scene was ordered and on September 2, after a period of leave in England and a parade to commemorate 200 years of existence, the Battalion sailed for its old wartime battleground, Cyrenaica, a province of the new Libya.

Derna, on the coast, was its base, a patch of green with the desert all about it. It was well-situated, strategically, for the Battalion's role of 'Fire Brigade'; it was out of the way, yet near enough for speedy intervention in any of the trouble spots that were liable to explode in the Middle East.

The details of the many political upsets of the region were never understood by the soldiers who were sent to cool them off: their role was to restore what no one seemed to want—order and tranquillity. The angry mobs in the streets seemed an essential prerequisite in Middle East political manœuvres, but they resulted in many innocent deaths and much economic waste. The soldiers were told to stop it.

At the Baraimi Oasis in the Trucial Oman States, and on the island of Bahrein, companies of the Battalion swept in at crucial moments and restored order. But as 1955 passed and 1956 drew on, the Middle East cauldron continued to bubble and the assumption by Gamal Abdul Nasser of supreme power in Egypt did little to quench the flames.

The 1st Battalion did not become involved in the troubles that attended the nationalization of the Suez Canal; no British government would have drawn the young kingdom into the dispute by using its territory to launch an invasion of Egypt. The Battalion stood by, at 24-hours alert, while the whole unfortunate episode unfolded. Afterwards, as the autumn of 1956 approached, a new reorganization was set in motion that had a profound effect on The King's Royal Rifle Corps.

As a first stage, the 1st Battalion moved to Tripoli and the 2nd returned to England and was there disbanded. The 1st returned to England, in the autumn of 1958, and the next stage of the reorganization followed. In brief, it meant a much closer integration with the Rifle Brigade and the inclusion of the Oxfordshire and Buckinghamshire Light Infantry into the Green Jacket family. The Green Jackets Brigade was henceforth made up of: 1st Green Jackets, 43rd and 52nd, 2nd Green Jackets, The King's Royal Rifle Corps and 3rd Green Jackets, The Rifle Brigade. A new cap badge was designed which incorporated features from all three regiments.

In this way the special, separate formation of The King's Royal Rifles was merged into the Green Jacket Brigade although retaining its separate identity in every way. As recently as December 1965, there was a further reorganization and a speech at that time by the Commanding Officer reflects the spirit of the 200-year-old regiment. 'In this life,' he said, 'if you are sensible and particularly if you are young, you look forward and not back.'

The 60th had always done that, from the first days of its existence. One of their officers, attempting to explain why the Regiment was 'different', said recently: 'We try to

The 60th double past in quick time—rifles at the trail—Berlin 1961.

carry out our orders competently and efficiently without making a fuss about it, and the secret of doing that is painstaking preparation in advance.'

There was, of course, much more to it than that. The 60th pioneered the relationship between officers and men which insisted, as a prerequisite, that the men could think and could be trusted. The atmosphere in the officers' mess to this day has a 'family' flavour about it. On the mess kit there are no badges of rank and all commissioned ranks, with the single exception of the Colonel, are on a first name basis. Another officer writes:

> Why is the 60th different? The key lies in its history and the sign-posts are its origins in North America (the philosophy of Colonel Bouquet, who was a century ahead of his time in tactics and what we now call man-management, has persisted), and the experience in colonial warfare, with the German Jäger traditions of Baron Francis de Rothenburg. It was he who provided the green uniforms, bugle calls, Regimental March and the formal technique of skirmishing.

The stress on individual skill down through the years has had a decisive effect on the regimental 'personality'. The 'do or die' philosophy of the Regiment of the Line has always been subtly altered by the 60th to 'make the enemy die'.

One small example of this attitude was provided by the 'men of Calais' who spent so much of their time escaping or attempting to escape that nearly all of the unsuccessful ones ended up at Colditz, the maximum security prisoner-of-war camp. In the words of one officer 'they spent more of their time outside the wire than inside'.

There is no need to despair as the unique title of the Regiment blends with the Oxfordshire and Buckingham-shire Light Infantry and the Rifle Brigade. All share in the traditions of Sir John Moore and his innovations. The 'parentage' of the new Royal Green Jackets is impeccable, and the traditions of all three regiments will now blend in a broader stream. 'Swift and Bold', General Wolfe's description of the 60th Regiment of Foot, will surely continue as a state of mind, if not as an actual motto.

THE KING'S ROYAL RIFLE CORPS
Regimental March

'LUTZOW'S WILD CHASE'

Although 'Lutzow's Wild Chase' was originally set to music by Weber, it was found that the rhythm (composed apparently as a cavalry march) was not exactly suitable for a quick march so it was allegedly given to an enterprising Band Master who corrected the difficulty by eliminating all but a few bars of Lutzow and substituting Von Gerhriech's 'Yagersleben' although retaining the name of 'Lutzow's Wild Chase'. The march is reproduced from the piano score prepared by Band Master R. Rodgers in December 1960.

D.C.

D.C.

"NO REPEAT.

1755–56	Regiment founded in North America as The Royal Americans.
1758–60	Conquest of Canada—Battles of Louisburg and Quebec.
1762–75	Indian uprising suppressed—Battle of Bushy Run. Service in West Indies.
1775–1808	The American War of Independence—Defence of Savannah. Further West Indian duties.
1808–14	The Peninsular War. Vimiero, Rolica, Talavera, Busaco, Albuera, Badajos, Salamanca, Vitoria, Nive and Toulouse.
1814–48	Period of peace. Title of the Regiment changed to the 60th, The King's Royal Rifle Corps.
1848–49	Sikh War.
1851–53	Kaffir War.
1857–58	Indian Mutiny—Siege and recapture of Delhi.
1858–59	India—Rohilkund and Oudh.
1860	China War.
1861–70	Canadian frontier guarded during American Civil War.
1878–80	Afghan War.
1879	Zulu War.
1881–95	First Boer War—Egypt—India. Sinking of the *Warren Hastings*.
1899–1901	South African War—Defence and Relief of Ladysmith.

1903–04	Somaliland.
1914–18	The Great War. All battalions in France until 1916.
1916–18	3rd and 4th Battalions in Salonika.
1919–39	Russia, Palestine, India.
1939–45	The Second World War.

1st Battalion—Desert. Italy.

2nd Battalion—Calais. Desert. Italy. Normandy.

7th Battalion—Calais.

9th Battalion—Greece. Crete. Desert.

11th Battalion—Desert. Italy. Greece.

12th Battalion—Normandy.

1946–58	Middle East.
1959	Formation of the Green Jackets Brigade.